BEAUTIFUL
On RAW

_{un}*Cooked Creations*

D1009191

Tonya Zavasta

BR Publishing
P.O. Box 623
Cordova, TN 38088-0623
www.BeautifulOnRaw.com

Disclaimer

The information presented herein represents the view of the authors as of the date of publication. Every effort has been made to make this book as accurate as possible. It was written with the intention of providing information about the raw food lifestyle and giving the motivation to follow it. The ideas presented in this book have been tested with great success by the women featured in this book; however, if you are not ready to accept full responsibility for your actions, safety, and health, please do not follow these ideas.

The information contained herein is not intended as a diagnosis, cure, or treatment for any disease or ailment. Because changing one's diet for the better often produces initial cleansing reactions, readers are advised to educate themselves adequately and seek advice from a qualified health or medical professional when needed. Neither the author nor BR Publishing accepts liability or responsibility for any loss, injury, or damage allegedly arising from any information or suggestion in this book.

Cover design: Gavin Anderson
Layout: Gavin Anderson, Sterling Studios
Editors: Sharron K. Carrell and Wendy Griffin Anderson
Back cover copy: Robin Quinn
Additional recipe editing: Gina S. Houston
Featured dishes prepared by: Chef Regina Szwabo

Published by:

BR Publishing
P.O. Box 623
Cordova, TN 38088-0623

Library of Congress Cataloguing-in-Publication Data

Zavasta, Tonya.
    Beautiful on raw : uncooked creations / Tonya
Zavasta.
    p. cm.
    Includes index.
    ISBN-13: 978-0-9742434-2-9

    1. Raw food diet. 2. Aging—Prevention. 3. Beauty,
Personal. 4. Natural foods—Therapeutic use.   I. Title.

RM237.5.Z38 2005   613.2'6
                    QBI05-800255

Dedication

To plain, imperfect, and physically underprivileged women who dare to be beautiful. My mission is to bring more health and beauty to this world by helping one woman at a time.

Acknowledgements

My sincere appreciation to **Alissa Cohen, Amanda Waldner, Annette Larkins, Brenda Cobb, Gina S. Houston, Millan Chessman, Rhio, Rozalind Gruben, Shazzie,** and **Suzanne Alex Ferrara** for their willingness to participate in the interview and to contribute their knowledge and experience in the raw food lifestyle, particularly in achieving rawsome beauty. You are the heart of this book — each and every one of you.

It gives me great pleasure to thank **Regina Szwabo** for her invaluable assistance in putting together some of the more sophisticated recipes. While I alone am responsible for any mistakes in the recipes, it was, nevertheless, of great benefit to have this professional chef's insights in a field in which I cannot claim expertise. I trust that her superb culinary skills have vastly compensated for my own shortcomings. She puts her passion for raw foods, her professionalism learned in the Institute of Culinary Arts, and 25 years of culinary experience into producing state-of-the art dishes.

I am indebted to **Sharron K. Carrell** for compiling and organizing the research on the benefits of different ingredients used in the recipes. Her editorial genius helped me, a Russian immigrant, gain a better command of the English language.

I enjoyed hearing from the **many people around the world** who have found my first book, *Your Right to Be Beautiful,* helpful as they incorporated the principles that I outlined into their lifestyle to improve their health and appearance. I am deeply grateful for your encouragement, questions, and suggestions. Your correspondence became the catalyst for this new book.

My thanks to **Gavin Anderson** for his superb professionalism, stoic patience, and incredible creativity with the book's design from cover to cover.

Heartfelt thanks to **Wendy Griffin Anderson** for proofreading and for wearing an editing hat as well, making this a better book through her editorial brilliance.

I am grateful to **Robin Quinn** for working with the back cover copy and skillfully nailing down what this book is all about.

I also wish to express my warmest gratitude to my son **Nick Zavastitsa, Jr.,** for adopting these healthy eating habits and being living proof that the raw food lifestyle works. I thank him, too, for being a constant source of encouragement to me.

And special thanks to my husband, **Nick Zavastitsa,** who continues to support my many projects, who constantly challenges me to search for the most convincing arguments in promoting my lifestyle, and who engages me in many thought-provoking discussions on the subject of raw foods.

Contents

Introduction

Beautiful on Raw: unCooked Creations, like my first book, *Your Right to Be Beautiful: How to Halt the Train of Aging and Meet the Most Beautiful You,* is based on many years of experience and observation, and is intended to meet the specific needs of women. It should be read as a companion to the first book. They are essentially a two-volume set — the first one deals with the *whys* and this one deals with the *hows.*

For some people, being gravely ill and without viable alternatives becomes a good incentive to start the raw food diet, but, for other people, a lack of motivation is the real problem. Many women have told me that they would not consider going raw for their health — they would just take medication. They would, however, do it for beauty — because there is no pill for beauty. For many, going raw is a better solution to finding their natural beauty than the unnatural process of plastic surgery or cosmetic procedures which are not only dangerous, painful, and sometimes fatal, but also are detrimental to general health. My goal has been to reach those women who will not "go raw" for health, but who will do it for beauty. Clearly, beauty is a great impetus. This goal does not, however, preclude men; the raw food diet is just as beneficial for them — it just makes them handsome instead of beautiful.

In my first book *Your Right to Be Beautiful* I told my story of transformation on the raw food lifestyle: from sick to vigorous, from aging to youthful, from plain-looking to beautiful. When I set out to write *Beautiful on Raw,* I had two primary objectives: to prove that I am not the only one who benefited from the raw food lifestyle and to present recipes from my own collection designed to help during the transitional stage.

People at my seminars often ask, "What if you are the only one fortunate enough to achieve beauty through the raw food lifestyle?" In other words, what if I were the exception? I had researched enough during my writing of the first book to know that I was not unique, so I set out to put this concern to rest and to offer encouragement to all the women who wanted to be beautiful.

I searched for women from all over the world who had achieved remarkable results from the raw food lifestyle. I asked them to share their secrets. I wanted stories and pictures from these women that would prove that I was not alone in having my life changed. I am including, along with my own interview, interviews with ten of these women who, like me, now dedicate their lives to promoting this wonderful lifestyle. I am sure you will benefit immensely from their experience and insights.

Since I wrote my first book, many people have asked me for my recipes. There are many excellent recipe collections available but I have tried to build mine around the simple transitional recipes that celebrate basic "from scratch" ingredients. Together with "to live by" recipes, this book emphasizes the benefits of 100 ingredients, most of them common but some unusual and little-known outside the raw food world or the specific culture that uses them.

I am not a chef, nor do I claim to be one. I never liked to cook, so for me one of the attractions of raw food was the ultimate simplicity. The longer I am on the diet, the less I require traditional food substitutes and the more I depend on simply juicing and eating small amounts of fruit, nuts, or seeds. My recipes are primarily for everyday use. My priority was to introduce my readers to nourishing dishes that did not sacrifice taste while they adapted to a new diet.

Another strong consideration for me was to present easily digested recipes because the change to raw food can be disruptive to a system raised on heavy, unhealthy cooked food. If one kind of nut is sufficient in a recipe, I never suggest using two different kinds. Where one type of spice will do, I will not use two. I do not use garlic and onion together because it compromises the digestive process. I have also tried to keep my recipes as simple as possible in terms of preparation and time.

For example, PRIMAVERA PISTACHIO PÂTÉ ON ROMAINE LETTUCE can be made in minutes. In the beginning, most novices depend on juices and salads. This gourmet sandwich is an excellent first step away from the ordinary salad. *Primavera* means spring, and this recipe is a first-rate way to enjoy spring on your table all year. It is easy to prepare but makes a sophisticated looking meal.

Another example is "BETTER THAN CHOCOLATE" MOUSSE, which is nourishing and loaded with nutrients. It is a healthy substitute for chocolate lovers. Coconut, bananas, and tahini make it a high-protein, high-fiber, high-energy shake that will keep you satisfied for hours. It is going to be your secret weapon against the ever-aggressive sweet tooth. Probably the hardest step in going raw is giving up sugar entirely. Sugar is insidious. Like salt, it appears in almost all prepared foods and is difficult to give up.

I have also included several more elaborate dishes, both for fun and to be creative in preparing a special treat for yourself and your family. As you can tell from the illustrations, some of these can be very glamorous. The reason is twofold: to help you make the transition by having attractive foods and to have attractive foods to help others deal with the transition. These are recipes that create a splash at parties and potlucks and make the statement that raw food is just as desirable as cooked.

In CLEVER CARROT CAKE, for instance, a guilt-inducing traditional cake has been transformed into a raw creation devoid of forbidden calories. Its intense nourishment, opulent appearance, and celestial taste always elicits cries of "It tastes better than baked!"

Fresh apples and pears are combined with fluffy macadamia cheese for a unique dessert in LAYERED APPLE PIE. In contrast to mushy, sugar-loaded traditional pies, this one is crisp, colorful, and fragrant with the luscious scent of green apples. The unaltered fruit colors and flavors guarantee that the nutritional value has not been destroyed. No sugar, no flour, and no butter — only wholesome goodness! Your perception of apple pie will be changed forever.

I used all of these recipes during my transition to the raw food lifestyle. Initially, recipes are very important. Food preparation is such a part of the cooked lifestyle that the simple act of making something highly structured fulfills a basic subliminal need. Using the more involved recipes in this book will carry you through that step.

You are going to give up cooked food, which is very heavy. When you begin the transition, the absence of this consistent heaviness is easily mistaken for hunger. It makes you uncomfortable because it is an unfamiliar sensation. My recipes serve as a means to fool the body's senses by looking and tasting familiar but offering much better nutrition. Initially you experience the need to feel full again, and that is why good recipes are crucial whether you stick to the lifestyle or not.

As your body becomes smarter and more accustomed to the changes you are introducing, it will direct you toward consuming less food, and that food will be of the very best quality. No matter how incredible it might sound to a beginner, the day will come when you will no longer care for recipes. At first you cannot stand the lightness that consumption of the raw foods produces, but, after several years on this lifestyle it is fullness that becomes insufferable.

As your body becomes more and more acclimated to the raw food diet, you will find that you prefer eating simple "mono meals" and will use fewer and fewer recipes. Keeping this in mind, I have tried to go beyond recipes to explore the benefits of the ingredients. A handful of soaked nuts is better than the best fruit-nut cake we can ever make. A bowl of blueberries by itself is always better than any blend or smoothie made from them.

Begin your adventure by reading the interviews I have included and then begin to change your life, your health, and your appearance with *Beautiful on Raw: unCooked Creations.*

Tonya Zavasta

Testimonials:
Raw Transformation

After (47 years old)

Tonya Zavasta

I have started writing a regular column, "Raw Beauty," for *Get Fresh!* magazine (*www.fresh-network.com*). I am including excerpts of an interview that they did with me in order to answer some of the questions you may have — along with some others that they didn't ask.

Where do you come from and where do you live now?

I was born in the former Soviet Union. My husband's family had wanted to immigrate to America for generations, and we were able to do so in 1991.

How many times have you circled the sun?

47. But, in 1997, the raw food lifestyle created a wormhole that reversed the direction of my orbit.

How young do people say you look, and how young do you feel?

My favorite comment is when people find out that I have been married for 25 years. They are always incredulous: "No way! Did you get married when you were five?" It's hard to say how young I feel, because I spent my youth feeling and looking less than my best. If I were going to guess, I'd say that I feel like I am 21 — old enough to be past the roller-coaster of adolescence, but young enough to be looking into the future with excitement and anticipation.

What led you to this lifestyle?

I have a very special appreciation for health and beauty because, growing up, I did not have either one of them. I was born in the former Soviet Union with bilateral hip defects and one leg shorter than the other. Growing with this infirmity all my life, I dreamed of walking normally. In 1997, advances in orthopedic science raised my hopes of addressing my congenital hip problems. There was a good chance that my limp could be corrected through extensive hip replacement surgeries. Having been through several previous operations, I knew how much anesthetics undermine one's health and appearance. Here I was with my lifetime dream about to be fulfilled, but that very fulfillment would leave me aging and ailing. I wanted a way to offset the devastating effects of multiple operations. The search for health led me first to the vegetarian diet, then vegan, and finally the raw food lifestyle.

I came to realize that the raw food diet offered the best solution to all of my problems. I really did not expect the dramatic changes that I experienced. I was just looking for a way to survive multiple operations without becoming an old, sick, and unhappy woman. I certainly got that, but the results far exceeded my modest expectations.

What is your professional background?

I earned a master's in Mechanical Engineering when I lived in Russia, and earned a master's in mathematics at the University of Memphis after we came to America. I taught mathematics and physics at the college and high school levels. I was admitted to the University's doctorate program at about the same time as I began to experiment with raw foods.

The possibilities of the raw food diet seemed endless, and I wanted to learn everything about it. But mathematics is a demanding mistress. It would not allow me to have another interest on the side. My fascination with what I was discovering took over my studies at the University. The results I was getting were so intriguing that I gave up my postgraduate mathematical studies (to the complete consternation of my family and friends) and immersed myself in researching the raw food lifestyle. The relationship between health and appearance became my special interest. *Your Right To Be Beautiful* is a reflection of this journey.

Is there a particular day or event that signified the starting point in your journey?

Oh, yes! I remember that day distinctly. I was still in the doctoral program in mathematical studies at the University of Memphis. One day, a renowned female professor visited the class to present a lecture on her research in some area of theoretical mathematics. It doesn't matter what it was; doctoral students themselves were barely able to comprehend her brilliance. What was significant was the effect that it had on me and the future course of my life.

She was in her seventies and looked sick and decrepit. Random patches of hair sprang up on her balding scalp. I was on the first row and was nearly overcome by the dreadful smell emanating from her. It was as though she were already dead and decaying even as her ingenious mind continued to function in complicated mathematical formulae. The contrast between her intellect and her appearance was intensified by the beautiful calculations she was writing on the board with an arthritic, liver-spotted hand.

Watching her was almost painful. I looked around. The body language of the audience mirrored my own reaction. It seemed everyone wanted her to leave the podium. Everyone was uncomfortable. As she presented her lecture, I found myself unable to follow her logic because I was staring in dismay at what could be my future. As beauty-conscious as I was, it scared me. I thought at that moment that senility would be a blessing compared to having an acute mind encased in crumbling ruins. In fact, if she had been senile, I would have been less judgmental about her looks.

At the time, I was too terrified of seeing myself in her to be charitable, or even rational. Most people at her age do not display such a mighty intellect, so how could it be that this mind did not tell her to improve her physical well-being. I was dismayed: such preoccupation with the development of the mind and such neglect of the physical body. Exalting the mind to the mortification of the body seemed very wrong to me.

The idea that she could not help her condition did not even cross my mind. I thought that at least some of this lofty intellect could have been used to research how to improve her health. All proof of her superior intelligence, all display of knowledge, seemed useless to me if it was not used to take care of her body. I knew that, if it were me, I would fight. I wouldn't be trying to produce another mathematical theorem for posterity; I would be seeking the solution to improving my health and appearance. Suddenly I realized that she wasn't wrong. I was. I was in the wrong field of research. She loved mathematics more than anything else in the world. She had forsaken everything, even her very self, to contribute to her favorite discipline.

It was obvious that my passion was misplaced. I was not meant to be a mathematician. For me, cherishing both mind and body was the most powerful objective, something worth a lifetime pursuit. At that moment I made my choice: Mathematics was in good hands; I, on the other hand, had to get out fast and find a way not to end up like her. I never went back to classes. Since then, I have discovered that the raw food lifestyle creates a loophole in the age-old assumption that "the spirit is willing, but the flesh is weak" and I have met attractive, vibrant women far older than she was. However, at the time, she was the catalyst.

How are your books different from other books about beauty?

I am not your typical author. Most beauty books are written by former beauty queens who have already capitalized on getting lucky in the looks lottery. By contrast, I was a plain woman, and disabled to boot. Like most plain women, I wanted to be beautiful. In my heart I always knew that the day would come when I would be able to walk without a limp. I just wanted to find a way to look youthful and beautiful when it happened.

When women compliment me on my appearance, and on my complexion in particular, I always say that even though I am immensely happy with the results I have gotten on the raw food diet, *their* transformation will be even more striking. If I was able to fulfill my dream despite adversity and being over the age of 40, then any woman — every woman — can fulfill her dream of being beautiful.

Did you find it easy to eat a raw diet in the early stages? What did you find difficult and what helped you the most?

Like everyone, I made several false starts. Cooked food is as difficult to give up as alcohol or nicotine, and sometimes people backslide. It requires determination to keep going. The hardest thing, of course, was chocolate. For almost everyone, chocolate is love. In my case, it was further imprinted on my psyche by the fact that my mother had worked in a chocolate factory, and my girlhood traumas were comforted by her gifts of chocolate.

It is not easy to eat raw at first. It can be extremely frustrating and requires intense discipline at all times. While it is not easy, it is, ultimately, simple. It is only difficult to the extent that we are still trying to change our habits and conditioning. Be aware that you will probably fall off the raw wagon many times. You may become discouraged, but if you persist, it will become easier, and then effortless.

How long have you been eating a raw food diet and what does your diet look like now?

I have been 100 percent raw since 1997. I now eat better quality food and less quantity. The longer I stay raw, the less food I need to sustain and satisfy me, and the better I look and feel. A few things are musts: vegetable juice once or twice daily and green salads with seaweed. The fruits I eat vary.

I try not to eat after 3 P.M. I get a refreshing night's sleep that way. The stomach is made of muscles, and late eating makes it work hard at night. Eating late suppresses the release of human growth hormone, which is credited with the rejuvenation of the body, because the body is secreting insulin to digest food. Having a period of time when the stomach is empty helps to shrink the protruding stomach that comes from constant eating.

What did you eat and drink today? Is this a typical day for you?

I had green vegetable juice at 7 A.M. Then I had another vegetable juice and a handful of soaked nuts at 11:00 A.M. At 3 P.M., I had a bowl of salad (tomatoes, red bell pepper, and dulse) with tahini dressing. This is an ideal day for me. If I do not eat after 3 P.M., I will awaken euphoric the next morning. I love it.

When I am having a hard day, I need comfort foods — just like everyone else. My comfort foods are fruits and berries. But I am much better off if I do not eat between my basic meals.

If I really want to indulge myself, I make my favorite dessert, "Better Than Chocolate" Mousse. In a regular blender or Vita-Mix, I combine two ripe bananas, two teaspoons raw black tahini, two rounded teaspoons raw carob and a pinch of stevia (ground leaf). I add some coconut water, depending on how thick I want it to be, and blend until smooth. This dessert is only for mature tastes. If you have never used stevia, you can add two dates. As a recovered chocoholic, I try to stay away from dried fruits because they trigger my sweet tooth. However, I ate a lot of dates when I first gave up refined sugar.

In what ways has becoming beautiful through a raw vegan diet changed your life?

Someone once said that you cannot appreciate happiness until you have experienced unhappiness. Because I initially suffered from an infirmity and then adopted the raw food lifestyle, I am in the unique position of having experienced something that does not happen very often. I went from feeling like a freak to feeling beautiful. It was an incredible transformation. I would gladly go through everything again just to experience the way I am now.

I now feel that much of my success is the response to my improved looks. And my new self-confidence improves my looks even more. I have found a "juvenescent" diet! The raw food lifestyle is the best thing that ever happened to me. At age 47, I am enjoying the best health and appearance ever. Hardly a day goes by without someone telling me that I am beautiful! If I am dreaming, don't wake me up!

How long would you say it took for you to see really visible improvements in your appearance? Would you say your appearance is still improving even now?

I saw visible differences within the first three months. My features became sleeker and more refined. Changes are still happening, but they are less dramatic now. Perhaps more importantly, I am holding the ground I gained almost eight years ago. I started to look younger almost immediately, and I do not think I have aged at all.

What non-physical benefits have you experienced through eating a raw vegan diet (e.g. emotional, intellectual, spiritual, flowering of talents, work-related, etc.)?

All of a sudden I started discovering talents I never thought I possessed. I started to write, took up public speaking, and began to sing at church — things I had never done before.

I am very focused. I am much stronger emotionally. I never suffer from depression, and I actually enjoy solving problems instead of letting them overwhelm me.

My personality changed. The goodness coming into my body as food brought gratitude to my soul and intensified my desire to share this lifestyle with others.

Who is your book written for?

Women like me. Plain women, imperfect women, women who long to be beautiful. Women who always wanted to be beautiful, but who gave up on beauty as completely unattainable. My book is also for women who look to dermabrasion and face lifts, collagen and Botox injections.

I also know who my books are *not* for: women who are making a statement with their neglected appearance will not even open my book for fear of being contaminated by vanity. These are the people who, to paraphrase Cyril Scott, are vain about not being vain about their appearance. My advice to them is that if the diet improves their looks too much, they can always wear a sack over their heads.

What would you say to someone who wants to look beautiful but is experiencing inner tension because s/he has a niggling feeling that a desire to become beautiful is vain, especially when there are so many problems in the world that need attention?

My countryman, Dostoevsky, made the profound observation "Beauty saves the world." What relationship can the raw food lifestyle possibly have with anything? It has everything to do with your life, global issues, the alleviation of suffering, in making a difference. My books have very little, if anything, to do with superficial beauty. Beauty is how health and wholesomeness should present itself to the world. Start with yourself and you will be better equipped to handle the problems of the world. If you are happy within, you can change what is without.

Do you feel you are in any way dependent upon being beautiful for your happiness?

Let's clarify what happiness is. Happiness means different things for different people. But we all agree that happiness is a by-product — it is what we feel when we succeed in what we love to do. For me it is growth: professional, physical, intellectual, spiritual. Happiness reveals itself as something pleasant in contrast to something that is not pleasant, so it is a reaction to improvement in the conditions of life. To feel happy, you must be able to remember unhappiness. In this sense, Rawsome Beauty brings happiness because it is continuous improvement. Conventional beauty can never enjoy this aspect of life. Happiness does not come from what we get easily; it is the aftertaste of satisfaction that comes after the achievement of a difficult task that demanded our best.

I discovered that losing gray hair and eye bags made me happy. In this sense, I can say that beauty does make me happy. I was very aware of my blessings, even before my transformation. I have a loving husband, a caring son, and a new life in a great country. Internally, I believe my newfound beauty made me feel that I truly deserve my blessings. It made me more comfortable with my bounty.

I have a growing sense of authenticity about my appearance. It is not arrogant to be appreciative of the changes I am going through. Nor is it narcissistic to feel good about myself, and about my appearance in particular. Being anything short of our natural best makes us frustrated and unhappy. The farther I am from my real self, the unhappier I will be; the closer I am, the happier I will be. I came to the realization that I am "wonderfully and beautifully made," and it is not my doing; appreciation is the natural response of anyone who realizes this truth. The result of becoming my true self is stupendous. My newfound health and beauty allowed me to live with a security, a confidence, and an inner peace.

Do you truly believe that anybody can become beautiful through a raw diet, or is it necessary to have "the basics" of beauty in terms of features and bone structure to begin with?

In achieving Rawsome Beauty, "the basics" of beauty give the recipient only a minute advantage. As you get older, how tall or how blonde you were born becomes irrelevant. After 40, a glowing complexion is far more important than long legs. Full, shining hair is more important than any particular color. Clear eyes become a much bigger asset than eyes of a certain size. After 40, any waistline is an achievement. Any proportion is a plus, not just 36-24-36. It is, nevertheless, good to know that features and bone structure do improve dramatically on the raw food diet.

The raw food movement recently got a celebrity infusion. Carol Alt wrote a book: *Eating in the Raw. Life* magazine calls her "the next million dollar face" and *Playboy* crowned her with the title "the most beautiful woman in the world." When she was racing cars, playing tennis, and shooting movies, I was fighting to be able to walk. When she was showing her gorgeous body to the world, I was hiding mine from my own husband. Where she valued beauty because it helped her achieve good things in life, I craved beauty as the only thing that could validate my existence. She came to the raw food lifestyle to preserve her most precious asset; I came to it as a way to achieve the beauty that would make my burdens bearable.

Deep down, I think I look just as good as she does. Even if I lose some credibility with you by saying this, even if you think I am living in cloud-cuckoo-land, you have to agree that most people over 40 do not feel as content in their looks. Blame it on raw foods. It will give you sky high confidence.

How about socializing?

Adjustments have to be made. I have become very good at making the best of almost any situation, but it does require discipline and ingenuity. My husband and I recently came back from a ten-day Caribbean cruise celebrating our twenty-fifth wedding anniversary. On the ship there was over-abundance of cooked food meals but good fresh produce was scarce. My solution? I ate watermelon for breakfast, lunch, and dinner. The doctor at our table kept telling me, "Tonya, with all this watermelon and no protein, you are going to wet your bed."

I was the talk of the cruise. The waiters called me The Watermelon Lady. I loved it! It gave me a chance to illustrate my position. After ten days, I never looked or felt better! Since I am at my optimal weight, I did not lose even a pound. But I did miss good, quality raw foods. I could not wait to get back to the car where I kept one organic apple! Nothing ever tasted more delicious!

We enjoyed the cruise, but we both agreed that from now on we will go on healthy vacations only. Drinking, eating to satiety, and partying all night are just not my type of fun. Raw foods constitute my essence now. My life and my very being are saturated by the practice, science, and philosophy of the raw foods lifestyle. I tend to gravitate to health conscious people who are most likely to be at yoga and raw food retreats and juice fasting resorts.

How much water do you drink?

Because I have vegetable juices once or twice per day as well as blueberries, watermelon, and coconut water, I get plenty of biologically pure water. I drink distilled water on the days I perform a water fast.

Since I carved my niche in the raw food community by studying how the raw food diet improves physical appearance, I am especially attuned to how raw food people look. I've noticed that people who always carry around a bottle of water usually have slightly visible eye bags. Eye bags are an indication that the kidneys are overburdened.

The raw food diet includes fruits and vegetables as well as soaked nuts and seeds, all of which are 70 to 85 percent water. Adding copious amounts of water like the recommended 6 to 8 glasses is too much of a good thing. There is actually a condition called water toxicity when sodium levels and other body salts, or electrolytes, in the blood become too diluted. This causes the sodium levels to drop and the brain to swell. An extreme case of such a condition occurred in Britain, when *The Times* reported a 23-year-old man going into a coma for four days after a 21-day diet of fruit, vegetables, juice, and water. He was drinking at least 5 liters of water a day.

What kind of exercise do you do?

While writing my first book, I regularly exercised in the gym. One day I was frustrated that my newly reconstructed hip muscles were not responding as quickly as I wanted them to. I decided to shock them and did 100 repetitions on a hip abduction machine. It was a big mistake: I developed bursitis in my left hip, a nasty connective tissue injury which takes years to heal.

I went to see an orthopedic doctor. He strongly suggested a cortisone shot. It did not help even for an hour. $600 less in my purse (because of my artificial hips I am uninsurable), and I was back where I started: on my own. I began searching the Internet. One person with a similar condition wrote that yoga helped him, so I decided to try it.

I will never forget my first day at yoga class. My poses were atrocious. My balance was nonexistent, stretching was extremely difficult, and the embarrassment was nearly unbearable. I even had to wipe away the occasional tear as it rolled down my cheek. What was I doing there in the first place? With two artificial hips, I felt like a freak on the midway at an old-time carnival. I was sure everyone was thinking the same thing. Only by sheer willpower did I finish the class.

After I got to know my class better, a lady told me I was an inspiration to her. She said she was doing her poses better just because I was there. This unexpected encouragement gave me another reason to keep attending, and I was gradually able to relax, which helped my condition to improve dramatically. Now I walk beautifully without pain or a limp.

In my yoga class, I always use a chair to help me with the poses. People in my class already know about it and none of the regular attendees will encroach on my chair. Recently, a new lady joined our class. She started to put her clothes on my chair. I told her I needed to use it for myself. At the end of the class she came up to me and asked, "Do you need the chair to achieve a deeper stretch?" I said, "Oh, no. I need the chair because I have two artificial hips!" She looked astonished, "No, you don't." I said, "Yes, I do!" "No, you don't." "Yes, I do!" It was when she said: "It cannot be!" that I began to doubt it myself.

There seem to be many similarities between yoga and the raw food diet in the way they affect the body. Yoga books describe the same experiences that I have from the raw food diet. It both purifies and heals your body. It has powerful therapeutic effects in dealing with physical and psychological problems. It promotes radiant health.

Both practices bring a liberating, energizing, and exhilarating feeling. Yoga increases strength, stamina, and flexibility. It releases tension and relieves pain. It enhances your looks, and improves your posture as well as your skin and muscle tone. Practicing yoga brings vitality into your life. In short, it enhances your experience of life. Yoga and the raw food diet make you more alive. Each practice complements the other and brings many of the same physical and mental benefits. I think that yoga should be an integral part of the raw food lifestyle.

What is your opinion on supplements?

If you have a deficiency, you must take a supplement for your deficiency, but I think that using supplements to ensure health is irresponsible. Any supplement taken for a prolonged time will create an imbalance that will aggravate another problem.

Today's science knows much more than it knew yesterday, so last year's supplements are inferior to the ones on the market today. And tomorrow's will have what is missing from today's. Every day, some vital new component or necessity for health is discovered.

Boron is the latest discovery among vital nutrients. The process of trying to emulate nature is endless. Ignorance has no beginning, but it has an end. Knowledge, on the other hand, has a beginning but no end. There are infinitely more needs to be discovered. Therefore, no man-made supplement can ever be good enough. When you use raw organic produce, you benefit from cellular communication and balance without knowing it.

The myth is that it is virtually impossible to eat enough food to get all the nutrients the body needs on a daily basis, so taking multivitamin supplements is the healthy alternative. This idea is not true if you are on the raw food diet.

I did very well my first six years without taking any supplements on a regular basis. However, I did try some of the more popular ones among the raw food people: MSM, Spirulina, and so on. I really did not notice any dramatic differences. After achieving a perfectly balanced dietary regimen, my body was so healthy and balanced that I was receiving everything I needed without any supplementation. I reached the pinnacle of health on my own, but there is nothing wrong with experimenting.

Several months ago, I read an article by Gabriel Cousens. It said that about 80 percent of vegans and raw food people could develop B_{12} deficiency. However, the other 20 percent do not develop a B_{12} deficiency. I believe that I am in this 20 percent because I have optimized the 100 percent raw food diet for myself.

Even though my blood work showed no deficiency, I recently started to take a B_{12} supplement. Why? Just for my peace of mind. For me it was either take B_{12} or have regular blood tests done. After enduring multiple operations, I have a strong aversion to any medical procedures. But this is the only supplement I take!

Don't you get bored eating only raw food?

On the raw food diet I don't graze in the garden, dig up the squirrel's nuts, or dine out at the birdfeeder. I simply learned new preparation techniques that allowed me to create nutritious meals. You have to agree that the variety even on the cooked diet comes from vegetable side dishes. There are hundreds of different kinds of fruits and veggies, nuts and seeds with a variety of tastes and flavors. If I combine only two or three ingredients at each meal, then the number of dish combinations is endless.

One might think some of your claims in your book are exaggerated. What can you say to that?

Some people might think that I come across as too bold with my claims. In reality, I noticed that any words I use are not strong enough to describe the experiences that come about on this diet. I insist that the raw food lifestyle delivers not only everything I promised, but much more than I could possibly describe using even the most sensational words in the English language. As an example, the word "rawsome" flowered from the raw food community for the simple reason there was no right word to convey this particular degree of good. In other words, my promises of benefits on the Rawsome Diet pale in comparison to the richness of the actual results you will experience.

Many people find it difficult to change a way of eating that has been socially accepted for generations. What is your advice?

Let me offer an analogy. Many people, myself included, immigrated to America. Was it worth it? Absolutely! Was it challenging? Of course! We had to learn a new language and a new culture, and we had to struggle with the problem of leaving our families behind. It is the same with the raw food diet. Transition is difficult, whether it is coming to economically advanced America or adopting a nutritiously abundant lifestyle. Is it worth it? Absolutely! However, just like leaving your native country, it is not for everyone. This remarkable dietary regimen is for the most adventurous of us, for those who will accept nothing less than the best for our lives.

Questionnaire

The response to my book, *Your Right to Be Beautiful: The Miracle of Raw Foods,* was very positive. For my next project I wanted to write *Beautiful On Raw: UnCooked Creations,* but I didn't want it to be just a collection of recipes.

I decided to enlist the help of women in the raw food movement who brought their own brand of dedication, beauty, femininity, and grace to the lifestyle. I wanted to glamorize it and make it attractive to mainstream women by sharing other success stories. My goal was to show that the raw food diet is a viable lifestyle choice that leads to optimal health and the best possible appearance.

I asked each of the women ten questions and requested that they provide before and after photos. Some women answered each question meticulously, but others had their own distinctive writing styles that did not conform strictly to the order of things. I have tried to let them speak in their own voices without repeating the questions for each interview. Here are the questions I sent them. I hope you enjoy their responses and follow their advice.

INTERVIEW QUESTIONS:

What brought you to this lifestyle? How long have you been on it?

What changes in appearance have you noticed since going on the raw food diet? Please, the more details the better. Include before and after pictures if possible.

How do you feel about your appearance? Were you considered beautiful when you were growing up?

Do you feel that you look your very best? If yes, how does if affect your self-esteem and confidence? If not, what do you think is preventing you from being the Most Beautiful You?

Do you have any special beauty secrets you would like to share?

What is your attitude towards cosmetics. If you do wear make-up, what are your favorites (brands, etc.)?

How would you describe your style? Has your choice of make-up, clothes, hairstyle, etc. changed because of the raw food lifestyle and the changes it brought about in your appearance?

What is your attitude towards aging? Do you feel that the raw food lifestyle has made you look younger than you are? How do you respond to looking younger?

Patricia Bragg, daughter of the legendary Paul Bragg, never tells her age, calling herself "ageless." She is carrying on the pioneering work begun by her father, who opened the nation's first health food store. She is co-author of many health books, including **The Miracle of Fasting.** *What is your attitude towards revealing your age? Do you tell it freely or do you share the opinion that "Women and music should never be dated"? If you tell, how do others react?*

Please share your favorite raw food recipe, the one you consider your trademark and always make for special occasions.

Before (29 years old)

After (35 years old)

Shazzie

I had been searching for the answer to ill health and depression all my life, and it cleverly eluded me until about four years ago, when I was 30. I'd tried everything to make myself feel good, and nothing did. Finding out about raw food was my wildest dream come true.

I'd been a vegetarian from 16 and a vegan from 18. Even though I didn't eat junk food, most of my food was cooked and high in pasta, potatoes, and rice. When I found out about raw food, I thought to myself, "No wonder I'm always ill!"

One really big thing I notice in myself and other healthy raw fooders is that they have this glow. Hollywood stars really have to work on their glows, and we have it immediately with no effort! Look at Juliano and David Wolfe; they'd both glow in the dark! That's something I found in myself, too. I used to have sallow skin, spots, rough bits, peely bits, jowls, and no rosy cheeks. My hormones used to be all over the place, and I got really patchy skin on my face.

Now my skin's really smooth all over. I rarely get a spot, and I glow! I could never imagine going out without foundation a few years ago. I was paranoid about it, and it got worse in the sun. After going raw, I never saw that again. I put foundation on my face one night after being raw a while and thought it made me look dead. I took it off again!

I lost a lot of weight and kept it off without effort. I went a bit too skinny for a while, but this was just because I was relentlessly detoxing. I'm now a really healthy weight, and I get only good comments about my body. As for other changes, my bones are straightening a bit. I think this is going to be a long process, as it's major structural work for my body. My face is a bit straighter than it was, and my teeth feel straighter, too. My breasts changed! From being downturned "lemons" they turned up and filled out a bit. That was amazing! I have tons less cellulite now, too.

These changes all just happened. I didn't have to work on any of them. That's what's so great about being healthy raw, your body just gets the chance to do all those things it wanted to before but couldn't because it was diverting its energy elsewhere and didn't have the right materials.

I used to look so down all the time — because I was! Now I just radiate happiness. My jowls went within weeks. I have just one tiny wrinkle at the age of 35, and I smile so much now! I normally love the way I look!

I love the bits that aren't considered normal as much as the other bits, because it's all me. It's not about my physical attributes; it's about my vibe. When my vibe is good, and I'm enjoying life, I look ten times better than when I let things get on top of me! I can see this in photos. Some photos shine, and others are so bad I don't think they're me! I don't know what people thought of me when I was growing up. Maybe they thought I was pretty but so miserable or distant that I was a bit odd. I really don't know.

Mostly I think I look my best. Like I said, on those rare off days I look weird and like someone else. Mostly I think I look the best I can. My serenity helps that. Of course, feeling good and feeling like you look good affects your confidence. And it's such an easy thing to alter. If there's one thing on your body that you really don't like, just tell it over and over that you love it. Love will break through anything.

Wearing an inner smile is the best beauty secret! If you feel happy, deep joy, serene and peaceful, you'll naturally have an inner smile. People could come up to you and go "Have you had a face-lift?" just because you stop carrying your baggage around in your wrinkles! I rarely wear makeup these days. When I do, it's some of the more ethical brands, but I've never found makeup so natural that I'd want to recommend it. I still get my hair dyed, and go to an Aveda salon for that. I did go *au naturel* with my hair colour, and, in Spain, that was easy, as the sun made it blonde. However, British Mouse isn't my favorite shade, so I have it altered!

You know, people are always asking me, "Have you got colored contact lenses in?" because my eyes went such a bright shade of blue after going raw. They used to be that bright, and over the years they dimmed, like everything else in my life. Now they've lit up again, and they glow so much that people often don't believe they're real!

I'm an Aquarian, so my style is totally eccentric. Barely anything I have matches, and I don't care! I buy something if I think it's pretty, and it doesn't even matter if it suits me. I used to hang my clothes on the wall like works of art. My boyfriend keeps trying to do something about my appearance, but I think I'm a bit of a lost cause!

Raw foodism caused me to experiment a lot with everything in my life, and clothes were no exception. I tried the hemp thing, but I never find anything except baggy clothes that don't feel right on me. I love the whole idea of hemp clothes, and if a fashion designer ran with it and made more stylish clothes, it could hit the mainstream. That'd be so fab, as agro-clothes are so detrimental to our beautiful world.

I don't have an issue with ageing. My family has good genes in that department, so I do look younger than many people my age. Being raw got rid of my jowls and frown marks, which then made me look even younger! I also know that being raw gave me a younger attitude, and that helps greatly, too. It's not like I'm irresponsible, but I don't carry the weight of the world on my shoulders like I used to. When you promote raw foodism as heavily as I do, you have to look younger/fitter/happier than average, otherwise your best selling point isn't there!

As far as telling my age, I don't care what people know about me. My whole life is on the Internet; what difference will announcing a number make? It's always a great talking point when I mention my age, as most people go "Oh, what's your secret?" Then I (gently) sock it to them!

Choosing a recipe. Oh, that's tough! I've published over 230 recipes. How can I choose one? Errr. Okay. I'll choose Corn Ring as it's so pretty and versatile.

You can make this very pretty with the flowers and leaves. If you can't get flowers, then decorate it with your imagination. Try other fillings such as hummus, salsa or seed cheese.

Corn Ring

Mixture from Flax & Corn Crackers
1 serving of guacamole
1 bunch of rocket
1 handful of alfalfa sprouts
1 bunch of chives
¼ cucumber
10 macadamia nuts
Chive, rocket, or other edible flowers

Make the corn rings in advance (they keep for a couple of weeks), by following the Flax & Corn Crackers recipe. Once you're at the dough stage, spread it into two large (dinner plate-sized) circles and dehydrate. After three to four hours, cut a hole into one of the circles with a biscuit cutter. Continue to dehydrate until firm but still slightly flexible (usually about 8 hours in total).

For the salad, chop the cucumber into small chunks, chop the chives, and mix together all ingredients except the corn rings, nuts, and guacamole.

Just before serving, sandwich the rings together with half of the guacamole. Make sure the circle with the hole is on the top.

Pile the salad inside the center hole. Spread the rest of the guacamole on top and add the macadamia nuts on top of the whole thing. Decorate with any leftover flowers and herbs.

Flax & Corn Crackers

These are so easy to make and are a good bread substitute when first lightening your diet. These recipes can be varied so much that I've just written a basic one and then offered a few of the many alternative ingredients. Crackers go well with all salads, soups, cheeses — in fact most savory recipes. They're excellent for buffets and doubting relatives alike.

2 cobs of sweet corn
1 clove of garlic
2 cups flax seed
2 dessert spoons sesame oil

Crush the garlic and strip the corn. Put the flax seed in the blender and blend until they're broken. Add all the other ingredients and blend until the mixture is fluffy. Spoon out the mixture onto dehydrating trays, and flatten until about 1cm thick (they will get much flatter as they dry). Dehydrate until crisp.

Variations:
Add ingredients such as chopped herbs (chives are really good), sea salt, chopped tomatoes, peppers, chili, onion, mushroom, or mustard powder to the mixture. Try putting the mixture into different bowls and adding different flavors to each one. To identify them, decorate the tops. For example, on the tomato one add a slice of tomato on the top; on the chive one add a halved chive flower bud.

Guacamole:
2 avocados, peeled and stoned
1 or ½ medium red chili, de-seeded
1 clove of garlic
2 tomatoes

Chop the garlic and chili, then put all ingredients in a food processor and blend until smooth, but still with little bits in it. For a chunkier guacamole, don't process one of the avocados — instead, dice it and mix it in afterwards.

Location: England

Phone: (International) +44-08700-113-119

Website: *www.Shazzie.com*

Books: *Shazzie's Detox Delights*
       Detox Your World

Shazzie also has DVDs and does personal appearances.

After (62 years old)

Annette Larkins

I became a vegetarian in 1963 at age 21. It was not due to the influence of any animal rights group; I had not even met a vegetarian at that time. Religion was not an issue. I was nutritionally ignorant; so better health was not the reason. I simply began to abhor the taste, touch, and smell of animal flesh, and — get this — my husband owned a butcher shop at the time.

Although it seemed to happen suddenly, in retrospect, I realize that there were previous subconscious factors preparing me for a lifestyle change that I would never have thought possible, given my background as an animal flesh eater.

One such factor, I recall, was eating ham hocks and momentarily being repulsed by the jiggling fat hanging from under the skin of this hog meat. However, the thought was brief; this was food on which I had been raised, and I had no plans for eating meals without meat. In fact, in my mind, I loved meat, and a meal without animal flesh was not a real meal. So, I continued to eat it.

Although I was nutritionally uninformed during the initial stages, I began to read material that led me further down the dietary path. I eventually abstained from refined sugar and flour; later I omitted egg and dairy products.

It seemed a natural progression that twenty years ago my "Journey To Health" finally culminated in the Kingdom of Living Foods, live and raw — where live is king, raw is queen, and I am a willing and loyal subject.

In my late teens, I weighed 130 pounds. After giving birth to my two sons, I became acquainted with the yo-yo syndrome — fluctuating up and down. I was never fat, but, had I continued the pattern of gaining and losing, I would eventually have been humongous.

I always had a small waist, but when I became a raw foodist, it got even smaller. After a while, I noticed that the yo-yo syndrome ceased. The reason, of course, is that when one eats properly, the cells are satisfied instead of tantalized, decreasing the desire to overeat. Being on a raw food diet actually puts one in balance, leveling the body to where it needs to be. My weight leveled to 110 pounds. I feel great, and have more energy than I need. I am always saying that if I could bottle my energy and sell it, we could all be millionaires.

I am not comfortable self-critiquing my appearance. However, I always endeavor to look my best, and I feel that beauty begins within. Growing up, I received many compliments regarding my physical appearance. An example of how people respond to my appearance these days was noted in a recent visit to a farm area where I purchase seeds and plugs to plant in my home garden. The owner, after witnessing my love of planting said, "Annette, you are a peasant farm girl in a movie star's body." Raw foods have allowed me to maintain a physical posture with the passing of time that I might not have had otherwise.

It is part of my lifestyle to coordinate my wardrobe. Accessories — even umbrellas and hand fans — must match. Everything must match. As a rule, I wear one color, which is really eye-catching. Again, I dress to please myself, but it does create comments, even from little children. My fashion style is generated from a psychological compilation dictating a sense of self; it has nothing to do with the wonderful, raw food lifestyle.

I take pride in my appearance, and although I do it for myself, the positive public feedback is very rewarding. When I walk out of my door looking my best, I feel ready for the world — I hold my head high, walk erect, strut my strut, and am confident that I can interact with whomever I meet.

I am not sold on creams and lotions and magic potions for beautification. We hear about avocado or banana facials, applying lemon juice to the skin to lighten areas, and scrubs to exfoliate. There is nothing wrong with performing these regimens. I, on the other hand, prefer to eat my raw avocado and banana, and drink my lemon juice, and I find that a natural shedding of the skin occurs periodically.

One hint I have to share is that I keep a spray bottle of distilled water with a few drops of some essential oil: rose, neroli, myrrh, or any oil that's good for the skin. I sometimes spray this on my face to cool off when hot and at the same time hydrate my skin.

Because I love color, I love makeup. Makeup certainly adds color and excitement to the total package of one's appearance, but less is better than more. I usually use the brand name Fashion Fair, which is designed especially for black skin, but sometimes I dabble in formulating my own makeup from raw materials including beeswax and essential oils.

As I age chronologically, I feel privileged. I have the best of both worlds. I have the fruitfulness of youth because I am sustaining a youthful appearance, youthful attitude, and a youthful vibrancy attributed to the young. And I also have the wisdom that comes with age. Could it be any better? I believe the raw rood lifestyle (including sunshine, positive attitude, proper rest, and exercise) has definitely heightened my existence. As for exercise, walking and freestyle dancing are my favorites. It is important that we choose an activity we like, and just move that body!

I am proud to be 62 years young. I love telling my age because doing so inspires young people to strive to become ageless instead of giving in to calendar years, and older people are motivated to make changes to better themselves, changes that were previously thought impossible. When the older generation questions, "But isn't it too late for me?" I tell them, "It ain't over till it's over." Keep in mind that it will be wonderful to reach 120 years, provided that we are psychologically, physiologically, and spiritually sound. Otherwise, what's it all about?

One of my favorite recipe combinations is Corn Chips with Salsa.

Corn Chips

10 ears fresh corn kernels
2 cups corn meal

Blend in blender until smooth. Spread onto dehydrator sheets, score into triangles, and dehydrate at 110°F until crisp.

Salsa:
1 each large green pepper, red pepper,
ripe tomato (quartered)
½ onion
½ jalapeño pepper
2 cloves garlic
a few sprigs of cilantro
1 lemon, juiced

With "S" blade, chop jalapeño and garlic first; pulse in other ingredients, adding tomato last. Eat with corn chips.

Residence: Florida

Alark Publications
P.O. Box 770097
Miami, Florida 33177

Telephone: 305-238-1169

E-mail: *annette@annettelarkins.com*

Website: *www.annettelarkins.com*

Books: *Journey to Health*

Annette has also done a 12-part television show which she hopes to syndicate.

Before (49 years old)

After (55 years old)

Dr. Brenda Cobb

I went on the diet in February 1999 after I was diagnosed with breast and cervical cancer. My doctor recommended surgery, chemotherapy, and radiation. I refused this treatment and searched for something that would help me to heal naturally. I was adamant about not doing the mainstream approach of surgery and drugs because my mother and my aunts who had cancer opted for surgery, chemotherapy, and radiation and, like so many others who have taken this approach, their cancers just came back with a vengeance. I knew that I did not want to go down that road by filling my body with toxic chemicals. I never believed that poisons could heal me.

I found out about Dr. Ann Wigmore and the Living Foods Lifestyle and when I read what it had done for others, I decided to adopt this program as my healing regime. In this particular lifestyle, it is much more than a diet and includes not only raw foods, but living foods as well. The living foods are those which are sprouted and growing when you eat them, i.e., mung bean sprouts, lentil sprouts, sunflower sprouts, buckwheat sprouts, etc.

When I began this lifestyle, I did it to get rid of breast and cervical cancer. In less than six months, I was cancer-free and all of my other symptoms completely disappeared — including depression, arthritis, migraine headaches, allergies, chronic fatigue, insomnia, bad skin, acid reflux, indigestion, and heartburn. I had yo-yo dieted for years, losing and then regaining the weight — plus more. I used to take pills for everything from headaches and allergies to acid reflux and insomnia.

I found, when I adopted the Living Foods Lifestyle to heal cancer, that all of the other "health problems" healed too. I used to take double handfuls of vitamins and minerals every day too, but, with this lifestyle, I haven't had the need to take any pills. I'm getting the nourishment I need from the food I eat. This has been a principle that I have stuck to: no need for extra vitamin and mineral supplements because I'm getting all the real nourishment I need from my real food.

Not only did my cancer completely go away in less than six months, but the extra benefits were that everything else healed and I looked and felt 20 years younger. My doctor was so amazed at my complete transformation that he wrote the foreword to my book, *The Living Foods Lifestyle.* This is the same doctor who insisted that I have surgery and chemo. Now, he sends his patients to my center so that I can help them heal naturally. It's amazing.

I lost over 70 pounds and went from a size 18-20 to a size 6-8. I look younger and have fewer wrinkles. I once had problems with acne, psoriasis, and eczema; now my skin is glowing and beautiful. My once dull eyes are now bright and clear, and my eyesight has improved so much that I don't have to wear the glasses that I wore for more than forty years. I look twenty years younger. Cellulite diminished.

I stopped coloring my hair when I learned about all the toxic chemicals in hair dyes and how they can contribute to poor health. My hair turned back from gray to its natural color and became thick and full of body. It even developed natural curl and waves like I had when I was a baby. It looked pretty funny when my gray hair began growing in dark. I had gray tips and dark roots, the opposite of what you usually see. It first changed color in the back, then the top and, last, the sides. I'm so glad I stopped coloring my hair so that I could experience the "youthing" that the Living Foods Lifestyle brings. Many people who have come to my Institute to heal a serious disease have reported that their hair has returned to its natural color.

I feel great about my appearance. I have confidence and I know I look better than I ever have. I was considered beautiful when I was growing up. In fact, I was a beauty queen, but over the years, as I gained more and more weight and became fatigued and old-looking, I didn't feel good about my appearance. Now I look and feel younger than ever. My whole countenance is improved. I feel good about how I look and it shows. My confidence is tremendous.

I know that I look my very best, and it gives me great confidence and self-esteem. I feel as if I can accomplish anything I set my mind to. Also, it attracts people to come and take my course at the Living Foods Institute because when they see how great I look and feel they want to experience the same thing for themselves.

There are lots of programs making huge promises to people, but they don't deliver what they say they will. I don't make any promises about what my lifestyle course will do for a person, but, time and again, people are amazed at their complete transformations. The only way to know what it will do for you is to do it and see for yourself.

My best advice: Drink lots of water and be sure that it is good filtered water. At home I use the Living Water System that filters out the harmful chemicals and toxic substances but keeps the minerals. It also oxygenates the water so it energizes the body more. More oxygen means more efficiency for the cells, organs, glands, and tissues. When I need to drink bottled water, I use Penta. It has smaller molecules which can be absorbed into the cells better than regular water. It is also oxygenated, which forces the molecules into the cells at a higher and more efficient rate.

Drink 1 to 2 ounces of wheatgrass juice every day. Use wheatgrass juice on your skin as an astringent and mask. It will tighten the skin and pull out impurities like blackheads and whiteheads. It's great for acne and blemishes and for softening and smoothing out the skin.

Eat 100 percent all organic fresh produce. Conventional produce is grown with and sprayed with chemicals which are toxic to the body. When the body is toxic it is reflected in the skin. Good skin comes from the inside out. It's only organic for me.

Do dry skin brushing daily to remove dead skin and the toxins that have been eliminated through the skin. Soak in Dead Sea salts and essential oils and a hot bath. This helps to pull toxins out of the skin. Use organic, therapeutic essential oils on the body. These act as medicines to the body to detox and rebuild. Each oil is directly related to a particular gland and organ of the body. I have created some special blends of oils for myself and my students. Essential oils are wonderful in helping the body to heal and maintain optimum health. When you use them, they are absorbed directly into the body through the skin.

Get regular colonics and do enemas at home to keep the colon clean. This will help with overall health and greatly improve the skin. After colonics and enemas, implant wheatgrass juice in the colon. Wheatgrass juice has every vitamin and mineral known to man, a full spectrum of all the amino acids, and more protein than all the meat and fish products — and it's cleansing and purifying to the blood. It is a miracle worker.

I don't really need cosmetics now because my skin looks so great on its own. I use to wear a lot of cosmetics and it took me forever to get ready to go out. Now I use organic almond and apricot oil to cleanse and moisturize my face. I have a natural glow about me so I don't need makeup base.

I use a little lipstick and sometimes a little blush. I get these from the health food store so that I know they don't have toxic chemicals in them. I don't have any particular favorite and am enjoying my low-maintenance, high-styled look. Many times, as women get older they tend to use more cosmetics to try to make themselves look younger, but it does exactly the opposite — it makes them look older and painted. Less is best when it comes to cosmetics, and a natural look is always preferable to a made-up look.

My style is youthful and modern. When I lost weight and healed I was more interested in my appearance and enjoyed dressing youthful and looking good. I changed my hairstyle into a short, spiked look which adds to my youthful appearance. I gave away or sold all of my black clothes. Nearly everything in my wardrobe was black before the Living Foods Lifestyle. I was trying to hide the weight, and I believe that the black reflected my depressed feelings.

Now I wear only color, and my closet is full of bright colors like orange, yellow, red, turquoise, gold, purple, and luscious greens. People comment all the time on how bright I look and how great the colors are on me. I have inspired many people to add color to their lives and get rid of the black. Colors are healing and energizing. I know which colors look best on me, and, if it's not a good color for me, then I don't buy it, no matter how good a deal it is. I dress for my age and don't try to look like a teenager, but at the same time my look is very youthful and fresh. I'm well-coordinated from head to toe and take pride in my appearance.

I believe that each age is wonderful. The older I get, the better I get. As I age I become wiser with more life experiences, and with the Living Foods Lifestyle, I don't have to worry about looking old because every day when I look at myself in the mirror I realize how young I am. It's amazing how people respond.

I have been on many television shows like CNN, ABC, NBC, CBS, FOX, and several cable channels since I began this lifestyle in 1999, and the producers, camera crews, and hosts always comment on the fact that every time they see me I look younger than the last time they saw me. I don't even realize the dramatic changes until I look at the older footage of the television appearances and see that it's dramatic and incredible. When people see me out in public when I'm giving seminars or workshops and many of my former students will see me, they always come up to me and say, "Wow, you look great! You look even better than the last time I saw you. This lifestyle really works, and you're a walking testimony to that."

I think positive and look at the bright side of every challenge. There are always blessings to be found in every situation, no matter how it may appear on the outside. Between the wonderful lifestyle and the great attitude, I'm a magnet for others. People want what I've got, so my classes are filled with people wanting to learn my secrets. Positive attitude is the answer, and everything I do I do with love! I believe that love can heal all things and that when we give love in everything we do, we receive many blessings back.

I love it when people tell me I look younger. People usually guess that I'm in my 30s. I turned 55 on May 31, 2004, and I'm proud of that. I feel like a teenager inside, and it reflects on the outside. My attitude is a huge part of this. I love to tell my age. I'm proud of it. People like to guess how old I am and they always guess that I'm a lot younger. When I tell them my real age they can hardly believe it.

Even young people, teenagers, and young adults who are more critical of age will remark about how young I look. Recently I was at a family reunion and the children of a cousin of mine who was born on the same day and year as I was kept telling me how much younger I looked than their dad. They guessed my age to be 34. That's 21 years younger than I actually am.

I have before and after pictures that I show of myself when I do a seminar or am on television. When people see the photos and then look at the real me they can't believe that the photo is really me. They say things like, "You look like a whole new person." Well, I am a whole new person, and it happened from the inside out. There's nothing like the Living Foods Lifestyle to make you look and feel young. I will always tell my age!

As for my favorite recipe — now this is a tough one, as I have so many fabulous recipes. I was a gourmet cook before I adopted the Living Foods Lifestyle, and I believe that if we expect people to eat healthy then it has got to taste really good.

I have created the most interesting and delicious recipes, and even the die-hard cooked-food eaters lick my bowls clean. Children love my food, too, so it's easy to get the family to try healthy food. When I take my recipes to parties or entertain at home, I never tell people how healthy the food is. I just stand back and watch them devour the dishes. When they say, "This tastes too good to be healthy too," I just smile and say, "Who would've guessed that healthy eating could be this great?"

There are so many favorites, and my recipes are always big hits everywhere I serve them. But, if I have to choose just one, I'll choose my SPICY MARINATED GREENS. Like most of my recipes, they're simple to prepare and they are absolutely delicious. Also, I am big on educating people about the benefits of particular foods so, like Tonya in this book, I like to list some of the healing properties of the foods in a recipe.

When people understand the nutritional value of foods and why they are eating them, they are more motivated to include these wonderful foods in their diet.

Spicy Marinated Greens

6 cups kale
½ cup carrots, chopped
½ cup zucchini, chopped
½ cup red bell pepper
3 tablespoons chopped garlic
2 teaspoons cayenne pepper
2 tablespoons chopped ginger
½ cup lemon juice
2 tablespoons Nama Shoyu raw soy sauce
½ cup coconut oil

Chop the greens and other vegetables into very small pieces so they will be easier to digest. The food processor is great for this. Put all the ingredients into a bowl and toss well, until the liquid completely coats all the greens. If you like more juice in your greens, you can double the lemon juice, soy sauce, and coconut oil. You can eat this right away or put it in the refrigerator and let marinate. You can marinate from 2 hours to 24 hours. They get better the longer they marinate.

Location: Georgia

The Living Foods Institute
1530 Dekalb Avenue
Atlanta, GA 30307

Phone: (404) 524-4488

Email: *info@livingfoodsinstitute.com*

Website: *www.livingfoodsinstitute.com*

Books: *The Living Foods Lifestyle*

Brenda also does personal appearances and gives a 10-day course in the Living Foods Lifestyle. She was awarded an honorary cultural doctorate by the World University for Therapeutic Philosophy. She has created over 1000 recipes to date. Some of them are in her book *101 Raw and Living Food Recipes,* which can be ordered at *www.livingfoodsinstitute.com.*

After Pictures

Rhio

My first summer job, as a teenager, was in a fresh raw juice bar in downtown Los Angeles. As I worked at the bar, serving fresh juices and smoothies, I got to talk to the people who came in, and I realized that a whole world of information existed that I hadn't previously understood. I started making a connection between the food that we put into our bodies and the profound effect that it could have upon us. People with ulcers came to the juice bar for the cabbage juice. Others with kidney disease were taking home watermelon juice, and still others depended on a combination high in potassium, which consisted of carrot, celery, cucumber, spinach, and parsley juices.

Directly across from the juice bar, on the opposite side, was a small health food store. All day long I would serve juices and smoothies, and between customers, I would look across at this fascinating store with its intriguing books and strange products. Every week, when I collected my paycheck, I strolled across to the other side and bought books. I don't think I actually took home much money that summer, but I did take home books! Some of the books I bought were by Dr. Ann Wigmore. That is how I was introduced to the raw food diet.

I wish I could say that after discovering this wonderful information, I immediately converted to a raw lifestyle, but in those days, there was absolutely no support for it. During my early years, I went back and forth between raw and cooked food. I knew that raw was better, because I felt better when I ate it; but I was young, experimenting and learning.

Years later, after a traumatic experience, I gained a lot of weight from using food unwisely to try to tamp down my emotions. Eighty-eight extra pounds heavier, I realized that I had to get control of myself. Finally, I went on a fresh raw juice fast, with lots of exercise, and lost the weight. A powerful incentive had been provided by my sweetheart (life partner), who booked me at a club where I used to work as a singer, before I gained weight. The booking was six weeks away and it helped me to focus on losing the weight. Of course, I didn't lose all the weight before the gig started, but I did lose half of it. Afterward, I just kept going. I have been a dedicated raw food enthusiast since 1987.

As for changes in my appearance, my skin, which was always good, got even better. I never get pimples anymore. It's easier to maintain my weight. I come from a Latin background, and, in my family, the women tend to carry extra weight. I've been able to maintain a normal weight more easily since converting to a raw food diet. During childhood, I had two serious cavities in my teeth. As an adult, I lost those two teeth. However, since I went on the raw food diet, my teeth have stabilized and I have had no further cavities or any other problems with my teeth.

I feel good about my appearance. I echo David Wolfe's words, from his book, *Eating for Beauty,* where he stated that the human body is a beautiful work of art in progress. I was not considered beautiful until I reached my teen years. At least I never heard anyone call me beautiful. During my growing up years, I used to hear "she's pretty" or "she's cute." But in my teens, when I discovered boys ... and they discovered me... then I heard the word "beautiful."

As a work in progress, I don't feel that I've seen my best self yet, but I do feel good about where I am most of the time. What can shake my confidence temporarily is when people compare me unfavorably to the models in magazines who, though they are attractive, are very, very slender. Most of them are really underweight. As a singer in show business circles, sometimes I am made to feel inadequate because I am not so slender. I look too robust.

I like to look healthy and robust, but some people don't view me that way; rather they compare me to the images that are presented in the media as normal/favorable. Because of this, there were times when my confidence wavered, but soon afterward, I recaptured my good sense and again valued myself for my own unique look and individuality.

The best thing that you can do for your facial skin is to freeze it everyday. Ice cold water is very, very toning to the skin. I have read that Marilyn Monroe used to sit in a bathtub of ice cubes! I don't go that far, but I do use ice water on my face. In order to do so comfortably, you have to get a pair of thick rubber gloves from the hardware store; the object is to freeze your face, not your hands. Put four or five trays of ice cubes into a large bowl, fill the bowl with water and, using a washcloth, splash your face for five minutes with the ice water. Now, some people with very delicate skin might have to use caution, but I have found that ice water tones the skin like nothing else. After splashing, just let the water air-dry naturally on the skin.

I also carry a small plastic spray bottle filled with filtered water in my purse and I use it to spray my facial and neck skin several times a day. I do this because water is what holds moisture in the skin; living in our polluted cities dehydrates our skin. It's like the difference between a fresh apricot full of water and a dried apricot, devoid of water. Drinking lots of water throughout the day is also essential.

A very good technique for drawing blood up to nourish the face is to stand on your head or hang upside down. There is a piece of equipment available that allows you to hang upside down. Another simple practice involves using fruits and vegetables on the outside of the body as well as the inside. For example, you could use fresh grape or apple juice as a moisturizer. They are both excellent for the skin, as well as very economical. Some of these beauty rituals are probably not for everyone, but they are effective.

I believe in the value of cosmetics to enhance a woman's appearance, and I do wear makeup. I find for myself, however, that less is more, so my complete makeup takes only five minutes. On a special occasion I might take more time. I use only a light powder on my skin, no base. Most of the makeup I use is for enhancing my eyes, which I think are one of my best features.

If I have a style, I've been unmindful of it up to this point. Now, finally, I am actually putting in some effort by experimenting more with clothing and hairstyles. I'm going to shoot some videos soon, so I figured I'd better get with it. I love having long hair, which I've been told is not very fashionable. I don't get my hair layered, so there's only so much one can do with it. I want to have waist length hair; I'm a couple of inches short of my goal. For me, long hair feels very romantic.

The raw food lifestyle will make anyone look more youthful — there is absolutely no doubt or question about it at all. And when you think about it, it makes so much sense. Everything you put into your body comes sun-blessed from Nature; there is nothing better that you can do for yourself, except to grow your own. And that is the next step in my raw evolution — growing my own, at least part of the year, here in New York State.

I love looking younger than I am, and previous bitter experiences now help me appreciate how wonderful this feels. When I was in my overweight phase, someone once asked if I was my boyfriend's mother. I cried for days — and after my tears dried, I did something about it.

I agree with Patricia Bragg about age. When people ask my age, I say that I'm an "adult, ageless." I believe that in today's world, people carry very negative attitudes towards aging. And they can usually point to the proof of their convictions. They would be very surprised to discover that many people, unhampered by foregone patterns and conclusions, can maintain youth into so-called old age.

To combat the prevalent negative impression of aging, I don't really associate any number of years with myself. People may put a number to me, but I don't do it myself, unless I'm compelled to in a legal situation or something. Human souls are ageless in that they may have lived many thousands of lifetimes anyway. So, in the long view, we truly are ageless, and the passage of time is just an artificial construct that humans have created here on earth. You can either buy into this outworn, non-serving construct or joyfully forge out as a pioneer in a new way of thinking and feeling. Future generations will benefit from inheriting the new model that we are setting in motion.

I've had many amusing experiences regarding age. Once, a policeman stopped me while I was driving and he refused to believe that my license was actually my license. He was kind of hostile at first, until I started telling him about my healthy food choices. Another time, at my birthday celebration, a small group of friends was standing around when my son came in with a friend. After greetings, my son's friend asked him where his mother was and when my son pointed to me, he was shocked! That was one of my best birthday presents, and it made me feel good.

One of my favorite recipes is also a prescription for beauty, inside and out.

Marinated Greens with Avocado

1 bunch collard greens
1 bunch Swiss chard
1 bunch Lacinto kale
3-4 tablespoons olive and flax seed oil
  mixed
juice of 2 lemons (or more)
2-4 garlic cloves (pressed)
½ teaspoon sea salt
1 avocado

Cut out the stems or ribs from all the greens and save for another use. (They are good for juicing and then using the juice as a base for a blender soup.)

Lay the large leaves on top of each other and then put the smaller kale leaves on top. (Do this in two batches, as there are too many leaves for one stack.) Fold the leaves in half and then roll the whole bunch into a tight roll. Starting at one end of the roll, cut into very thin slivers. Put the resulting ribbons into a large bowl.

Make a marinade of the oil, lemon, garlic, and sea salt. Toss the green ribbons with the marinade until well-coated. Put the greens into a bowl and on top of the greens place three heavy plates to weigh them down. Then place the bowl into the refrigerator overnight. The weight helps the marinade penetrate into the leaves.

Next day, before serving the greens, mash the avocado and, with your clean hands, massage the avocado into the greens. At this time, you might want to adjust the flavor by adding more lemon or sea salt, etc.

Without the avocado, the greens keep for 3 days in the refrigerator. After adding the avocado, serve immediately.

Serves 4-6.

Location: New York

Phone: 212-343-1152

Email: *rhotline@rawfoodinfo.com*

Website: *www.rawfoodinfo.com*

Books: *Hooked on Raw*

Rhio also gives personal consultations over the phone as well as doing personal appearances.

After

Rozalind Gruben,

A.H.S.I, R.S.A.

As far back as I can remember, I have felt an authentic and deep compassion for animal suffering. It was this emotional connection that resulted, at a young age, in my choosing a vegetarian, and then vegan, diet and lifestyle. Concerns with my health came somewhat later, mainly as a result of suffering from an extensive range of eating disorders. The discovery of a raw vegan diet literally saved my life. It provided me with the road to health, dietary and personal freedom. Cooked foods are addictive. Understanding this truth is paramount for anyone wanting to free themselves from disordered eating.

I discovered the science of health creation (known as Natural Hygiene) and the raw vegan diet twenty years ago. It took me about three years to fully transition to eating raw. I have now been eating an exclusively raw vegan diet for approximately seventeen years. During the past ten years, since meeting my beloved partner Dr. Douglas Graham, my diet has become further simplified, progressively lower in fat, and higher in carbohydrates (in the form of fruits). This has resulted in massive further improvements in my health, appearance, energy, and mental acuity.

After so many years of yo-yo dieting and obesity, the fact that my body fat has reduced to a healthy level and then stabilized continues to seem a miracle. The once densely blemished skin of my face, neck, and shoulders is now spot-free, smooth, and glowing with health. The skin on the rest of my body is also silky smooth and glowing, whereas, when I was eating cooked foods, it was rough and pimply. My nails, which were in the past a constant source of frustration as they flaked, split, and broke, now grow strong, long, and shapely.

Before I ate raw, sunburn and prickly heat were the result of even minimal sun exposure. Today, due to diet and lifestyle changes, my body is far less toxic as well as being abundant with the antioxidants provided by raw fruits and vegetables. The combination of these factors has resulted in my no longer suffering from prickly heat, even when spending time in the tropics. My skin easily tans to a beautiful golden brown.

Since eating raw, my body's natural odors vary from neutral to sweet. This is greatly different from my cooked days, when deodorants were a necessity even on cool days. Now, I can even go running in the heat of a summer's day and still smell as sweet as a rose! Due to the increase in energy I have experienced on a raw diet, I have the ability to be far more physically active, resulting in a fit body with toned and attractive contours.

In the past my concerns were centered on conforming to the "ideal" form of beauty as presented via the media, movie stars, models, and other cultural groups. In my teens I became an avid watcher of the Bond movies, not because I enjoyed or even followed the plots, but because I perceived that the type of beauty these women exuded guaranteed ulti-mate social acceptance and success.

My hunger for approval transferred itself to hunger for food, resulting in a journey that took me through a kaleido-scope of dietary agonies to finally arrive at obesity and des-peration. I was the proverbial princess locked in the tower of social conditioning. Year after year, I battled and struggled to set myself free from the self-imposed torture, but to no avail. Then one bright and sunny day, the healthy raw vegan diet arrived to rescue me, and I have not looked back since.

By growing through the experiences of my healing, I came to know the beauty of my own uniqueness, and the glory of standing proudly in my own physical authenticity. Today I celebrate the fact that my appearance bears no resemblance to anyone else's (including the Bond girls') and I live in the light of my own beauty rather than the shadow of cultural expectations.

I feel deeply grateful to my body for surviving all the abuse that I subjected it to in the past, and for its tenacious and ceaseless efforts to re-establish its vibrancy and beauty. I wear certain physical scars and other nuisances that I honor as records of my personal history, and embrace them as reminders of lessons learned. Most of all I appreciate that my appearance at any given time is unique to that moment; changing according to the degree that my psycho-emotional and physical needs are being met. This serves me as a valuable gauge by which to adjust my habits, behaviors, and thought processes.

No, I wasn't considered beautiful, or, if I was, it was not in any way that brought it to my awareness. I was led to believe that I was fat, which I accepted and, as a result, considered myself somewhat ugly. In reality I was only a slightly chubby child, but one who was on her way to eventual obesity. Each day of my childhood, I was learning more and more how to use food as an emotional analgesic.

I currently feel that I look the best that I can at any given time. Extensive traveling, undertaking transatlantic flights, and the emotional challenges inevitable to life take their toll on my energy, health, and beauty. I believe that perfection is not attainable within the realms of the human experience; there is always one note that is misplayed in every philharmonic performance. However, each day is rich with opportunities to create a personal symphony.

The subject of self-esteem is a complex one and, to me, fascinating.

Behind every manifestation lies an intention. In the past women have pursued beauty with an intention of submitting to a patriarchal dictation. In return, that dictation sank its claws into the self-esteem of the collective feminine. The evolving woman of today is busy re-seeding her intent. She is reclaiming her power and amplifying her own beauty in honor of herself.

Historically, the role of cook has kept women in the kitchen for hours and hours of their lives, resulting in their investing enormous time and energy trying to solve the health and beauty problems that result from eating such foods. The rebirth of the natural raw diet has come as a divine gift for women who are ready to rebirth themselves into the beauty of domestic and physical freedom.

My own self-esteem is no longer rooted in how I look or the approval of others, but rather in my capability to govern my own grace. The raw diet has provided me with this ability by removing a primary cause of physiological and psychological distress — cooked food. No longer do toxicity and physical disharmony drain my psyche, render me emotionally discordant, and prevent me from leading my life in ways that I can be proud of.

True beauty will always evade any woman who has crafted her appearance due to her reliance on it for self-esteem. Her appearance will be a skin deep and artificial façade, as mine was for nearly thirty years. I have since taken a 180-degree turn and reached a place whereby my appearance is simply the consequence of my self-esteem, rather than vice versa. In other words, my sense of self-worth expresses itself through the ways in which I nurture my body and present it to the world.

Health and beauty are created by more than diet alone. Factors such as physical activity, sleep, exposure to natural full spectrum sunlight, air quality, choices of thought and consequent emotional experiences, the expression of creativity and sexuality, and many other lifestyle habits are all powerful influences. Each and every person has stronger and weaker areas when it comes to how they meet the needs of their physical body and psycho-emotional self.

In my case, stress has previously been my weakest link. In the past, I have allowed the way that I process my world to place me under great mental and physical strain. This has taken its toll in many ways, including depriving me of sufficient sleep on many occasions. In recent times, I have made great strides in this respect and have developed new ways of nurturing myself emotionally. None of us can erase our pasts, and I am aware that my body would be all the more beautiful today were it not for the emotional traumas I have survived.

My understanding is that all aspects of life, from matter to form, are, in actuality, energy vibrating at a specific frequency. This being the case, I believe that beauty is the physical manifestation of the energies of love, health, and harmony. No matter how perfect a woman's curves, shapes, or covering, beauty will escape her if her heart is heavy with angst or resentment, her body loaded with toxins, or her nerves enervated.

Here is my recipe for beauty

- *Walk through life with fear behind you and love in front of you.*
- *Get sufficient quantity and quality of sleep.*
- *Move like a dancer (posture is the foundation of physical grace).*

> • *Eat beautiful raw plant foods that have been grown with love, in a healthy environment, and in a way that is harmonious with the Earth.*

Throughout human history, body and face painting has been used for purposes of beautification, ritual, symbolism, and a variety of other tribal purposes. To paint, anoint, or decorate the body can be an act of self-reverence, communication, or tribal or personal affirmation. Despite the origins of this behavior having been mostly lost to the collective consciousness of our modern day western culture, remnants of the underlying historical intentions remain. For some women, the use of makeup still serves today to meet their need for deep-rooted cultural association and ancestral connection.

The modern day use of makeup for establishment of tribal positioning is evident in our western society. The "New Age" woman is expected to be devoid of makeup; a woman joining in the corporate dance is expected to wear a minimal amount of eye color with an emphasis on lipstick; the beautician is expected to demonstrate use of the entire spectrum of products available.

Whatever the reason for using cosmetics, it becomes destructive behavior only if the intent behind its use is unloving (either to the self or to others), or when the substances used are obtained without reverence for others or the environment. Sometimes in life there is a fine balance between self-loving and self-destructive modes of behavior, and the use of makeup and other cosmetics provides us with one such example.

The application of makeup may enable a woman to more readily appreciate her physical beauty (thus feeling more confident) or enhance her way of bonding with her social group (thus feeling more secure). But makeup, to some degree, is always detrimental to the health of her skin and possibly her entire body.

Makeup may allow a woman to express her creativity in the painting of her own face or body, but at what price to the environment or other creatures of the Earth?

Each woman must weigh her needs, consider the implications of her actions, and then boldly embrace her truth.

There have been times in my life, before I discovered the health-creating raw vegan diet, that I wore a lot of makeup in an attempt to conceal my skin's many blemishes and detract the viewer's eye from my obese form. These days I am liberated from such challenges but, on certain occasions, such as appearing in front of an audience, I choose to use a little makeup. I use mascara and an eyebrow pencil, and sometimes a touch of silver eye shadow under my eyebrows.

I do this with the intention of amplifying my own beauty and of demonstrating my honor and respect for other people. I buy only products containing ingredients that have not been tested on animals. I also seek out cosmetic manufacturers that declare respect for human rights and use minimal packaging of an environmentally sound nature. I have yet to find a company that meets all of these requirements, but I continue to search.

One specific type of cosmetic product I would like to mention is deodorant. It has become culturally ingrained in us that this product is essential to our lives. The use of deodorant (both of an underarm and genital type) becomes totally unnecessary in the presence of a healthy diet and lifestyle, when a naturally sweet body odor is exuded. All commercially produced deodorants are highly noxious and, long term, significantly add to the body's toxic load, resulting in an exacerbation of the problem. It has been a great joy to me over the years to watch my cosmetic bag get smaller (and my purse bigger) as the raw vegan diet and lifestyle progressively rendered so much of what I previously classified as "essentials" redundant.

For me, "style" is a rich word filled with endless potential. It can relate to style of dress, style of speech, style of movement, style of nurturing, style of creativity, and so much more. Style can relate to all those aspects that are an outward demonstration of a woman's energy, intent, talents, and direction. Collectively, style can be a reflection of her unique way of experiencing and processing her world.

As I have evolved over the years, my own style has undergone many guises, and I select that word with deliberation, because "guises" accurately describes the many non-authentic ways that I presented myself to the world in the past. So numbed I was by the analgesic qualities of the cooked diet that I was largely out of touch with my feelings, emotions, and personal truths. I had no style, as I had no idea who I was. Any style I adopted was nothing more than a façade hiding chaos and personal disorientation beneath its corset.

In more recent times, the full beauty of my own style has risen to the surface and continues to become manifest in my way of dressing, speaking, and behaving. I believe authentic style can only ascend from an authentic fountain of personal truths. My personal evolution has taken me down many paths of discovery and connection, including that of my ancestry. My lineage is Celtic and my energy powerfully feminine. I am strongly connected to the primordial and to our Mother Gaia.

My clothing style has come to be a blend of those influences. Similar to the way concealing makeup will never replace a naturally healthy complexion, clothing can never convey beauty unless its style resonates with a woman's underlying essence. For a woman to exude her natural beauty, she needs to first know her truth, and that is not possible when she is numbed from it by a toxic diet.

Yes, my style has changed in various ways and for a variety of reasons. Before I discovered Natural Hygiene and the raw food diet, my skin was covered in blemishes, especially on my face. From the age of 16 I would spend copious amounts of time and money on concealers and face makeup. I also used eye makeup heavily to hide the puffiness and dark circles that were constantly present, and as an attempt to distract people from my obese body.

Nowadays I frequently receive compliments about the quality of my skin, and I do not wear any form of foundation makeup whatsoever. The puffiness and dark circles are but a memory, and I maintain a slender body. The only makeup I occasionally wear now is mascara with a light touch of eyebrow definer. My clothing choices have changed dramatically. Whereas before the primary directive was on disguising my obesity, I now delight in amplifying the natural lines and curves of my figure. When I was in my 20s I dreamed of having a body that I would not be ashamed of, one that would allow me to wear the clothes that I wanted to.

Today I have that body and am so confident with how it looks that I do not hesitate to go naked when it is appropriate. My hairstyle has also changed as a result of my diet and lifestyle. I no longer use my long hair to hide a fat and blemished face, but am able to sweep it up onto my head or dress it in any way that pleases me.

I ripen; I mature; I grow towards the light, and, in doing so, the love inside me becomes ever more available. I do not age, nor does anyone else. Does the owner of a car become wrinkled and malfunctioning as the car she drives yields to the forces of time and environment with rust and scratched paintwork? No, she remains unaffected other than being inconvenienced, as do we on a spiritual level as our body approaches the end of its service, eventually liberating us from the human dance. We are more than our physical body and the core essence of each one of us is ageless.

Do I look younger than I am — possibly so; younger than I used to look — definitely!

I not only feel younger but have evidence that I look younger too. On the rare occasions that I allow friends to view photographs of me taken twenty years ago, their exclamations are essentially the same: they are astounded by the comparison.

How do I respond to looking younger? That is an interesting question. I respond by spontaneously dressing in what I perceive to be an ageless way. I undertake physical challenges that I probably would not if I felt older. I associate with younger people freely and easily without feeling myself to be their elder. In summary, I do not feel too old to do anything I desire to do.

When asked what my age is I enquire if the person wishes to learn of my spiritual, mental, or physical age, or if they are simply seeking to know for how many years I have been living. In my view spiritual, mental, and physical age are all very different in everyone and are minimally influenced by the length of time a person has been living. I have met with people who have been living for only a couple of decades yet demonstrate themselves to be advanced spiritually.

In contrast I know of people who have grandchildren yet are more mentally agile than some teenagers. The dietary and lifestyle choices a person makes influence all three aspects of their aging. The raw vegan diet not only makes a massive contribution to the slowing down of physical aging on a cellular level, but it also supports superior mental processing, as well as facilitating the development and connection of spiritual awareness.

When asked my age I feel at ease and confident in my reply. I am currently entering my forty-fifth year of life, I have the physical age of approximately half my chronological years, a level of mental agility fit for any age, and a spiritual maturity that no longer depends on comparison to others in order to be measured. In my view, the phrase you quote about music and women is coming from the same voice that has suppressed women for centuries, one that treats them as secondary citizens of use only for the sexual pleasures of men. The fear behind the phrase is "once I lose my looks I am of no value." I choose never to subscribe to such sexism.

The reaction of others varies, but my somewhat complex reply is not generally expected and takes people by surprise. Some express that they thought I was chronologically older; some laugh raucously at my analytical response; some look pensive and thoughtful and say nothing; but mostly people simply smile and nod in a secretive sort of way as if I have told them some deep secret. My ages are no secret with me; I am naturally open and healthfully youthful.

My secret is to simply work up a true appetite with vigorous wild dancing then sit on a mountainside amongst spring flowers and drink coconut water before eating a ripe mamea. Ah — true bliss.

Location: England

HLI Vice President
1 Cassidy Place, New Town Road
Storrington, West Sussex, RH20 4EY,
England

Phone: 0-1903-746572

Email: *healthyunlimited@aol.com*

Website: *www.healthfullivingintl.com*

Books: *Introducing Fasting and Detoxification Programming*

Rozalind is an author, teacher, and lecturer who is on the board of Healthy Living International (HLI).

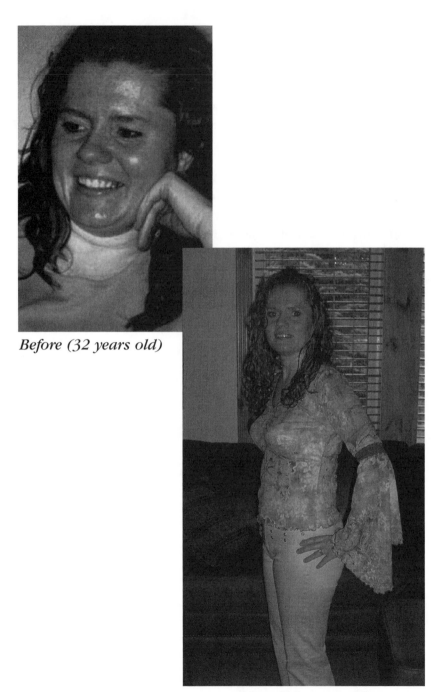

Before (32 years old)

After (34 years old)

Amanda Waldner

I have now been on the raw diet for almost two years, not always 100 percent. I have only been 100 percent for the past few months. I had a few slip-ups which got me not so much into eating cooked food as into eating some sugars and breads.

My search for the truth about health began when I was in high school, when I started suffering bladder infection after bladder infection. My mother took me to the doctor, where he prescribed more and more antibiotics each time. I remember times when I was on a round of antibiotics two or three times a month. It was never something my mother or I even thought twice about. We trusted the doctors and believed they knew what they were doing. And so week after week, month after month, for almost two years, I went to the doctor about this bladder problem that would not go away, no matter what the doctor prescribed.

I would later find out that a yeast infection in my bladder was causing all the havoc in my body. Because I kept feeding it antibiotics (which only makes yeast grow), I kept getting worse and worse until, finally, I could no longer attend school due to the pain and sickness. It was at this time that I started questioning the doctors and what they were doing, because I was not seeing any improvement — I was, in fact, getting worse all the time.

Over the years, my life went up and down and up and down. I would learn something about natural health, like dairy not being good for the body, and would apply it and notice a big improvement. Then, after feeling well for a while, I would have a bit of ice cream here and there, until I noticed that, once again, I wasn't feeling well. That would push me forward to learn more; then I would put into practice what I had learned and would go through the whole process of feeling better and then cheating all over again. I went on doing this for many years of my life, until I got pregnant with my first child. It was at this time that I was trying once again to be better with my eating.

While I was pregnant with my first son, I was trying to find a way of telling others the truth that I had learned about toxic chemicals. I decided to look up guestbooks on the internet — under "natural health," of course — and started leaving messages for people to see if that would help spread the word about toxic chemicals. That was when the truth hit me squarely in the face and changed my life.

I came across a website by someone named Tasha Ann and her site was all about Natural Hygiene and raw food. As I read the information on the site, I noticed that a lot of the things that I read were things that I knew, but when I read about *raw* food, something clicked inside of me and I said to myself, "Of course! This makes perfect sense!" I had known about the benefits of eating fruits and veggies for years, but never really even thought about eating an all-raw diet. This time I knew that I had found the answer. After the birth of my first son, I started putting into practice the laws of nature and started eating more and more raw food. And the more raw food I ate, the better I felt.

I didn't start eating raw food to become thin or beautiful; that just happened. This is the most incredible thing about raw food eating! As soon as I started eating raw food, I started losing weight, and, in fact, my first week of eating about 80 percent raw food I lost ten pounds. I stepped on the scale and nearly fell off when I saw that I had lost ten pounds, just like that, without even trying. In fact, I actually felt like I was eating a lot more in the beginning, and yet I still lost weight.

The next thing I noticed was unbelievable to me. One day I was checking out my weight loss in the mirror and turned my back to the mirror. I looked at my bottom. I nearly freaked right out, as I saw no cellulite on my bottom or my thighs. "Holy crap!" I said, unable to believe what I saw. Over and over again I kept looking at my backside in the mirror, then I would walk across the kitchen saying "I can't believe this...I just can't believe this!" Women try and try with pills and massage to get rid of those ugly dimples, all to no avail. I didn't even try to get rid of them. Just by changing my diet from cooked food to raw (and at this point I wasn't even 100 percent), those ugly dimples melted away. It has also been a wonder to see the puffiness in my body disappear. When I look at myself now, I look more youthful because my body isn't puffy and fat.

My eyes seemed to change quite a bit. I have had red, bloodshot eyes for years now, but after eating raw food, most of that redness in the eyes has gone. My nails are a lot stronger, too. I used to suffer from my nails splitting and breaking, and now they don't do that at all. My hair has changed as well. I used to wear my hair just one way most of the time, but now I like to wear it different ways. I like to let my hair be more free and bouncy rather than tight and "perfect" with spray.

My skin has improved greatly! I have noticed a tightness in my skin that I don't think I have had since I was a young girl. And, since I have started making green juice a part of my daily routine, the one thing that I hated most about myself — the large pores on my face — has started to clear up. For as long as I can remember, that has been the one thing that I would like to change about myself. I have always had such terribly large pores on my face that wearing makeup was a must because I was so embarrassed about them. Those large pores have decreased by over 50 percent since going raw and they keep getting smaller all the time. I feel so good about my appearance, and, the more I eat raw food, the better I feel about my appearance. I have a confidence about me now that allows me the opportunity to show others my beauty just by the way I present myself, which comes from the way I look and from the way I feel. Feeling clean on the inside will automatically make you feel beautiful on the outside. I feel empowered and strong!

I do not really know how others perceived me growing up, but I never felt as beautiful as most of the other girls. Maybe that was because I never seemed to get the guy that I liked or get asked out or got the flirting that the other girls seemed to get. I do not think I was unattractive at all, but I always felt less beautiful than most other girls. Now I feel better looking than I have felt in years and, though I still have a C-section tummy to get rid of, my body physically feels more beautiful than since my early teens. I feel my best is yet to come, but that it isn't far off.

My self-esteem and confidence are close to being the best they can be. I walk with a feeling of being beautiful and looking beautiful. I know that comes from feeling beautiful on the inside. I really feel that, though we feel beautiful on the outside, nothing makes your beauty shine to others like when you are clean and beautiful on the inside. It just radiates from you!

The only thing preventing me from being the most beautiful me that I can be is keeping steady with my workout routine. Having two little kids has made it difficult to find the time every day that I would like to have to exercise my body.

Body brushing and green juice are my beauty secrets. Green juice and body brushing make my skin glow and make it tight. They make me feel like I am shining from the inside so brightly that all of me is aglow. The only natural beauty tip I can give is kind of funny. I take a beet and cut it and then rub it across my lips to give them a natural pink color. Don't leave the juice on too long, though, or the pink may become quite bright.

I love cosmetics! I am one of those people who think cosmetics are great for enhancing the beauty of a woman and I love them. There are days during the summer where I just wear mascara and lip gloss and I feel gorgeous. Then there are days when I like to wear it all: mascara, eye liner, eyeshadow, foundation, blush, and lipstick. A little or a lot, I enjoy wearing cosmetics. My favorite brand of makeup is the Neways line called Leslie Dee Ann. I love the way it feels, but, more important, I love that their products do not contain any harmful or toxic chemicals.

My style is feminine beauty. Without question, I like long floral dresses with sandals and would love to wear more hats in the summer. I love to wear clothing that enhances my figure and makes it look as though I am the epitome of health and beauty. My choice of clothing has definitely changed since going raw and feeling more beautiful. I love to wear clothing that hugs my body a little more and clothing that is a bit more sexy. Not that I want to draw attention to myself, but rather that it just enhances my feeling of beauty and empowerment and the strength that makes me feel like a success.

I don't worry about aging at all. I feel better than I felt fifteen years ago and now, as I enter my mid 30s, I am excited for what will come in the future. Aging comes from how we feel more on the inside than how we look on the outside. When you feel healthy, you look healthy and you become healthier. The healthier you become, the healthier you want to become and will become. And when your health is optimal, no matter your age, you are going to feel young and beautiful.

Do I feel that the raw food lifestyle has made me look younger? Most definitely! I feel as though I am in my early 20s. Though I think I have always looked younger than I am, I feel younger; therefore, I believe I look younger. How do I respond to looking younger? With joy, joy, joy! I am 34 years old and loving every minute of it. I am not afraid to tell anyone my age and, in fact, I welcome people asking me my age. I love it when people do because almost always they will respond with "WOW, I thought you were younger than that!"

My favorite recipe is definitely...

Plum Pudding

2 cups plums, skins and pits removed
20 dates, soaked
1 banana
1 cup pecans

Put all of the ingredients in food processor and pulse until well-mixed but still a bit on the lumpy side. This is so terribly yummy!

Have a vibrant day!

Location: Canada

Email: *rawfooddiet@shaw.ca*

Website: *www.simplyrawsome.com*

Amanda and her husband have started the Rawesome web-site to help educate people on the raw food lifestyle.

After (64 years old)

Millan Chessman

I had a daughter when I was 36 years old and I knew I wanted to see her children, but I knew that if I did not take care of my health that was not going to happen. That was the turning point in my direction towards receiving optimum health. I knew much about internal cleansing but little about diet and its importance, so I had my ups and downs during this journey.

Since my mother and father were both Type II diabetics, I have struggled with sugar addictions — so weight increases occurred. I got off eating refined sugar and white flour by eating raisins on a daily basis when the cravings occurred.

Cleansing internally helped me make the changes I needed to obtain optimum health. I remember my grown son telling me "Mother, what you need to do is exercise and you will stay slender." Now, remember that at that time I was 50 years old and had not exercised a day in my life. But I listened to him and started aerobics. Today I do high impact step aerobics with the 20- and 30-year-olds and keep up with them. I work out six days a week for one hour each day and am completely addicted. I am slender and still get checked out by the young whippersnappers.

About fifteen years ago, I learned the importance of eliminating all animal products from my diet. That has made a huge difference in my health. My body no longer has a foul odor, nor does my elimination and gas. It has been so much easier keeping my weight off and my energy level dramatically improved.

When I was in my 20s, my bowels moved about once every five or six days. Now, at age 64, my bowels move two times daily. I attribute that to my diet and internal cleansings. I cleanse once each week internally.

When I was a child I was always overweight. I can remember being called "fatso" in junior high school, because I weighed 175 lbs. I was an ugly duckling growing up.

Now it is pretty incredible when a 30-year-old comes up to you during an aerobics class and says "you have got the tiniest waist. You have a wonderful figure." Believe me, when one lady says that to another lady, you know it's a compliment.

My confidence doesn't come so much from my appearance, but from the fact that I am accomplished in the determination to be healthy no matter what anyone else says. I know that my healthy lifestyle works.

You determine optimum health by how you look and how you feel. I have accomplished both. I am now married to a man who is 23 years younger than me. I have eight grandchildren. I fast 24 to 48 hours per week, drink fresh-squeezed carrot, beet, celery, spinach, parsley, and cucumber juice every day, and do seven-day fasts throughout the year. Now I eat only God-made foods, fruits, vegetables, grains, legumes, raw nuts, and seeds.

I brag about my age. It's even on my business card. That's a lot to brag about. Remember, Dr. Norman Walker lived to be 118 years old.

The only real beauty secret I want to share is going to sleep early and get up early. Studies have proven that sleep before midnight is more beneficial to the body. I need at least eight hours sleep. Yes, I wear makeup every day. It makes me look more beautiful, and I am all for that! I have to — and enjoy — purchasing my clothes where the teens shop. I can wear those sizes. I dress like a 20-year-old.

Because my ad showed my photo and age under it, a gentleman responded. He told me that his wife said, "Oh she lies about her age to get more business." (I am an alternative health practitioner.)

Tonya, I would be doing a disservice to your readers if I did not include the spiritual avenue I take that keeps me young and vibrant. God's word says that when we follow Him, He will give us a long and healthy life, including His wisdom. My confidence is not in myself, but in He who created me. He said He will give me **life and more abundantly**. I am so glad for that good news, because I accepted His Son, Jesus Christ, into my life twenty-five years ago and I now live to love others and not selfishly for myself only. I am grateful to now "acknowledge Him in all my ways and He directs my path."

Here is one of my favorite recipes.

Kale Delight

1 head of kale or chard
juice of one lemon
sea salt to taste
2 cloves garlic, crushed
¼ cup virgin olive oil
¼ cup red onion, chopped very fine

Remove vein of kale or chard. Tear leaves into small, bite-size pieces.

Mix lemon, salt, garlic, olive oil, and onion together first. Then add to kale or chard. Massage the greens well. You should feel the texture change and the volume should appear smaller. Marinate in a glass container, in the refrigerator, for 4 hours or overnight.

Enjoy!

Location: California

Phone: 1-619-562-5446

Email: *Millan@coloniccleanse.com*

Website: *www.coloniccleanse.com*

Books: *Stay Young & Healthy Through Internal Cleansing*

Millan is a certified health practitioner and lectures extensively.

After

Suzanne Alex Ferrara

I first learned about the power of raw food 30 years ago. As a young woman on my own, I began my first food experiment. I had never been taught that there was any connection between health and food. Left to my own devices, I ate pizza and drank cappuccinos almost exclusively. I began to experience serious digestive problems as well as constant pain in my lower right side.

The doctor put me on pain pills and antibiotics. Things got worse and stronger antibiotics were prescribed. When that did not work, an exploratory surgery was scheduled. After being given some sedatives on the morning of the surgery, a nurse casually mentioned that I was scheduled for a hysterectomy. That woke me up. When I was given the permission sheet to sign I wrote on it that they did not have my permission to remove my reproductive organs.

I dozed off and was abruptly awakened by an angry doctor asking me what was the meaning of this. In my drugged state I recall telling him if there was any growth in there that was not normal he could remove it as I feared cancer, but that the things that I was born with must remain, as I intended to be a mother one day.

Upon waking, I was informed that I had a cyst on my right ovary. It had been drained and my appendix, even though only slightly inflamed, had been removed. I was served steak for dinner that night. At this time a neighbor, Dona, came to visit. I was nearly hysterical about the way this doctor was treating me. She told me in a firm and calm voice that if I would eat like her I would never have to see this angry, hostile man again.

For the next two weeks I took the pills that were given to me and ate little but didn't change my basic bread, meat, and cheese style. At my check up, he informed me that the cyst was back and now it was bigger than before the surgery. The doctor raised his voice and looked like he was going to explode as he told me we would now have to schedule another surgery to do what he wanted to do in the beginning.

I went to Dona's house and began my raw food and juice therapy. I did not see another doctor until I was pregnant with my daughter ten years later. I had remained around 75 percent raw for all that time as well as fasted periodically. Six years ago I made the commitment to 100 percent but have since evolved to a place I call 99 percent because it allows me to have an occasional cooked vegetable in the winter.

The first year after the surgery, I consumed a diet of exclusively juice, fruit, and salad. I had not visited my brother in all that time, and he didn't recognize me as I stood at his door. I had always been plump. Not especially fat, but certainly plump. It was more than that though. The shape of my face, my posture, my skin had all changed. For the first time in my life people were telling me that I was beautiful. They called it beauty, but I knew it was radiant health.

At first the change in my appearance was a bit frightening. Guys would follow me and ask me to go out with them. I was focused on my fabulous state of well being and quite surprised at this new attention. As a child and a teenager in school I had been made fun of and called names. I don't think I was seriously ugly but it was quite apparent that my looks were not up to some standard. I thought the best I could hope for was to be somewhere in the middle so

I would not be picked on. The idea that I could be beautiful wasn't even a possibility to me.

I became aware of the benefits of attractiveness in a way that one who has always been attractive would never notice. People were nicer to me. Unfair as that may seem, it was true. I didn't get tickets from traffic cops. Sales people waited on me first. People went out of their way to be kind and friendly to me. After one amazing kindness offered by a stranger, I recall thinking that I should take very good care of this newfound beauty because its value was far greater than money.

I used my knowledge of herbs and raw food to keep my new look and health. In my early 40s, I realized that this jumping in and out of cooked food wasn't going to serve me well in the long run. If I intended to maintain my beauty, I would need to take it all the way. After becoming 100 percent raw, I experienced a new level of well being and, once again, even more attention. After removing bread and dairy from my diet completely, I saw the face in the mirror becoming younger and more refined. This new level brought with it a desire to share this knowledge. I had always had the gift of making food taste incredible, and I wanted to show people that it was not only easy, but could be better-tasting than the food you thought you would miss!

The path to the most beautiful you is a life-long experiment, and I am far from done. I don't want to stop aging; I want to reinvent it. At the time I am writing this, I am celebrating my fiftieth birthday and I can't help but notice that I have a better body and presence every year. I see no reason to stop now. I have come to think that what you think is far more important than we have as yet accepted. My work now as a personal trainer encompasses yoga, raw food, herbal treatments, and hypnotherapy. My current work with hypnotherapy is reveling in the possibilities of molding the appearance like a sculptor by clearing mental obstacles.

My most profound beauty secret is to love what you do, eat, and wear. I apply my extensive knowledge of herbs in my facials and bath therapies. Stress is the enemy. Don't take life so seriously. Laugh as much as you can. Above all, be flexible in body and mind. On an everyday level, I avoid makeup as I feel my skin likes to breathe, but light makeup is fun, and fun is good for the soul. My favorite facial is a clay mask with senna leaf powder, followed by a raw honey pack. I love the natural look but want a little flash with it. I use products that contain only vegetable dyes and no fragrances whenever possible.

Looking younger than you are can actually have some drawbacks. In our society, respect for accomplishments and wisdom are associated with age. If you look like a kid, people can assume that you are inexperienced and naïve. Mature men who are your intellectual equals may not consider that you would be interested in them. Young men are fun for a minute, but can lack the depth that age gives them.

I don't think about my age and often have to pause a moment to remember the actual number. Having birthdays and noting these numbers eventually becomes irrelevant and can cause you to associate with the examples of age that you saw growing up. I remember reading a story of some men trapped in a mine. Only one man had a watch. They all knew that they could only survive for 24 hours without outside air. The man with the watch also knew that it could take much longer than that for the rescue teams to reach then. He chose to tell everyone that only one hour had passed for every two hours. When they were rescued on the second day, the time-keeper was the only one who had died.

My work with hypnotherapy has reinforced my belief that what you *think* is true *becomes* true. One of my favorite things about giving hypnotherapy sessions is seeing the radiant beauty that emerges after one finishes a session. Lines and creases disappear and the skin glows. This is the facial of the future. Work from the inside out.

My favorite recipe is:

Avocado Heaven Soup

In the blender place:
one whole, ripe, pitted avocado
2 cloves of garlic
3 teaspoons tamari or Nama Shoyu
½ teaspoon thyme
⅛ teaspoon cayenne

Blend while adding enough warm water to make mixture the consistency of pea soup.

Location: California

Email: *suzannealex@excite.com*

Website: *http://suzannealexferrara.com*

Books: *The Raw Food Primer*

Alex is also an accomplished artist. Her work can be accessed through her website.

After Pictures

Alissa Cohen

I went raw about thirteen years ago, but it took me about seven years before I could make the commitment to stay raw. My transition was rocky at first. I had been vegetarian since I was 16, but I was eating a lot of processed junk foods. I figured since I wasn't eating meat, chicken, fish, or eggs, I must be healthier than most — but I was wrong! I developed chronic illnesses, bladder and yeast infections, and headaches, and I tired far too easily. I gained ten pounds and couldn't shed them. I was put on antibiotics, but the infections always returned — along with more prescriptions for drugs. I finally decided to get off the roller-coaster ride.

At first, I would be raw for a month or two, but peer pressure, cravings, and the like would lead me back to cooked food. I never felt as good when I ate cooked food. I finally had to make a decision. I started incorporating raw food into my business of personal holistic fitness and finding other people who were making great changes in their lives. I think a major problem for a lot of people is trying to fit into your past life once you have gone raw. You can't.

You have to create a new life and an environment that will support that life. That was the hardest thing for me. I had to let go of a lot of notions about how I was living my life. Once I got real with myself, it was easy to sort out the friendships, relationships, and work that did not suit me any longer. I had thought I was happy but I was just numbing myself with my drug of choice — cooked food — when things were not optimal for me. Once I decided to stay raw, a new life began.

I began to feel and look younger and younger. I noticed lines in my face smoothing out. My skin would be flaky and dry at different times of the year or oily and prone to break-outs other times. When I went 100 percent raw, my skin became soft and clear. My eyes became clear and sparkling. My hair, which always seemed dry and dull, became shiny and healthy. My face began to take on a whole different look, not just chiseled from losing weight but aglow and vibrantly healthy. I was always fighting to keep my weight at a certain point, but being raw has enabled me to stop worrying about that; my skin is tighter and more toned.

Most of all, there is something that is almost inexplicable really; it's like this inner feeling of peace and calm and optimal health that actually shows up on the outside when you are raw. People are drawn to it. It's not about conventional beauty but rather this certain energy that radiates out that draws people to you because you are radiating this true, healthy, finest self. It's nothing that makeup or a new hair-style could ever compare to!

I was told I was "cute" and "attractive" growing up but I never thought of myself as cute or attractive. I was always looking in magazines or at other women and trying to take pieces of their beauty and make it my own. I would try to "make myself up" — my hair, my makeup — to be what I thought *the* idea of beauty was. I dyed my hair a different color and wore lots of makeup. As attractive as I may have been without doing all of this to myself, I never "felt" beautiful. I was always looking outside of myself.

As I became raw, that all fell away; my inner beauty started to emerge. I like my appearance now. I like that I no longer try to fit into a certain stereotype of beauty. Being raw has allowed me to shed all of the "fake" things I did to myself that I thought was beauty. That saying, "beauty is more than skin deep," is true! I feel as though raw food has allowed me to tap into the power to be my true self and let my inner beauty show through. I don't think there is anything more attractive than seeing a woman totally in her power — feeling and knowing that she is a powerful woman and does not need to try to be like everyone else. That is true beauty.

Yes, I feel that I look my best. *My best.* I think that is so important to emphasize the *"my,"* because I think that whenever we try to be something we are not, it always comes across to some extent as looking fake, or not as great as if it were less beautiful by conventional standard but real to us, real to our true selves. Have you ever seen a woman who is by most standards gorgeous, but there is no radiance, no energy, no "oomph" there?

Then think about seeing a woman who by many standard may not be "beautiful" but there is just something about her; the way she carries herself, the way she exudes self confidence and this inner knowing, the way she shines when she walks into a room. That to me is the ultimate beauty! Knowing and feeling the power of life and love and joy. Feeling that and leaking that from your very being — wow! That is beauty!

So, of course, I think that self esteem and self confidence are linked to how we feel about ourselves. I have so much more of both of these things since going raw. It's hard not to have much more self esteem and self confidence when you know that you are taking care of yourself the best way possible and treating yourself in such a loving, caring way.

Beauty secrets? These are always changing! I love playing around with stuff to put on my face or hair, but lately I don't have much time to do that, so I really keep things simple. Also as the years go by since being raw, I rely less and less on these beauty secrets and more on just letting my "naturalness" show through!

A few things I do swear by though are:

1. **Never use shampoo!** *It will dry your hair and damage it. Use only conditioner to wash your hair.*
2. *Use honey to wash your face. It will tighten, tone, and clear your skin, leaving it smooth and moisturized!*
3. *Drink lots of water! You will look dehydrated and worn if you are not drinking enough water.*
4. *Swim in salt water whenever possible. Not only is it good for your skin, but it will revive your soul!*
5. *Work out every day! Not only will it keep your body feeling and looking good, but your mind will be clear, depression will lift, and you will get a natural rosy glow!*
6. *Meditate. It will erase wrinkles, clear negativity, and make you feel and look years younger.*

I think cosmetics are great. I don't think there is anything wrong with wearing makeup, but many times it is used to "cover up" what we don't like about ourselves. When you go raw, or at least when *I* went raw, I started to see that I didn't need it! It was amazing, I, who never went out of the house without makeup, now hated wearing it! It started to feel "fake" on my skin, like I was wearing a mask. I noticed that I actually looked better without all of that makeup on.

Again, I don't think there is anything "wrong" with wearing it, but I think I look better without it or with just a little bit of it. If I'm going somewhere special, I wear some, or if I'm taking pictures for something I put some on. But it is incredible how much your skin glows and how your face lights up when you're raw. It's hard to want to cover that up with makeup. Whenever I have makeup on now, after a few hours, I can't wait to come home and wash it off. I never, ever thought that would happen to me!

I don't really have a favorite brand. I used to use Aveda, but I'm not sure how "natural" they are. I try to use whatever natural ones I can from health food stores. I have even made my own using beet juice as lipstick, and then tried dehydrating the pulp for rouge.... It didn't work too well; maybe that will be my next project!

I would describe my style as *very* casual and laid back. When I'm at home, I am either working on my computer, taking a run down the beach, or jumping in the ocean or my Jacuzzi, so I'm usually in cut-off jeans or a sarong or nothing! I'm not big into clothes. I hate shopping, and I would prefer to be naked! I think a lot of raw fooders are like that, but I've always been that way, so I can't really claim it's from the raw food. But it does feel a lot more natural to lay out in the nude than have to put on a bathing suit or cover your body up in unnatural fibers. The thought of shopping in a crowded mall and being trapped in a store trying on clothes is horrifying for me!

Years ago I would make myself shop for the clothes I thought were *"in,"* but now I just can't bring myself to do it. I pick up things here and there that I see in little boutiques or funky, fun stores so that when I do go out in public I can look presentable. But it's not something I put a lot of thought into.

As far as hairstyle, yes, raw food has changed that drastically. This is one area I have always been tortured in! I use to be a hairdresser, many, many, moons ago! Actually I was a colorist for a top salon in Boston. I even went to London to study with Vidal Sassoon. (Yes, I know, that was another lifetime ago!) so I was always into changing my hair color and cutting my hair in different styles.

For many years I wanted to have long, blonde, straight hair. (Funny how we always want what we can't have — I will never have long, blonde, straight hair!) As I got older and got away from that profession, I was still always tortured by my curly, frizzy, dark hair. It always looked dry and brittle, no matter what I did to it. But when I went raw, it became shiny and healthy.

I stopped blow-drying it and adding handfuls of products to it and coloring it and now I'm at peace with my hair. (For those of you with bad hair, you know what I'm talking about!) I now love my hair and how it looks. It has relieved me of hours of stress having to style it every day to just make it look okay. I now let it air dry and I never put anything in it. (For those of you with unruly hair, I know what you are thinking, "I could never do that!" But you can!) Being raw has changed my hair texture, my skin tone, and the entire look of my face and body!

I am looking forward to getting older. I enjoy the wisdom and peace that come with aging. I'm more sure of myself and my decisions, and less self-conscious of who I am, what I do and say. There's a lot of freedom in that. Unfortunately, as many people age, there is often sickness and a feeling of our bodies breaking down — not feeling well — so it's hard to enjoy the feeling of freedom that naturally comes with getting older. But because I am raw, my body is healthy and free from sickness, disease, and uncomfortable aches and pains, I look and feel younger and younger every year and my mind is clear and happy and joyful, so I'm excited for every coming year.

I enjoy looking younger of course, but for me it's really only about how I feel within myself. Am I happy with myself? Am I living my authentic life? Do I feel good in my own skin? If I can answer "yes" to these questions then that's what's important. If other people think I look good for my age and that, in turn, influences more people to eat this way so they can heal themselves and live happy, full lives, then I am delighted to be a good influence and motivator for them.

I don't have a problem telling my age. I don't think I ever will. I think there's a problem with your own self-esteem when you don't want to tell your age. Why wouldn't you want to tell your age? I would think that if you don't want to tell your age, it's because you don't feel comfortable in your own skin. If you are proud of who you are, how you look, what you've accomplished in your life, what you are about, why wouldn't you want the world to know how long you've been here doing what you're doing??

I hope that I can be teaching people about this way of living for many years and that I will be able to say: "Look, I'm 90 and look how much energy, stamina, strength, beauty, and joy I have in my life; you can have this too at my age!" I think we all have the capacity to inspire and teach one another if we put ourselves out there. To me, hiding your age is hiding a part of yourself that should be celebrated, not rejected.

Oh boy! Favorite recipe! This is a hard one! Okay, here is my favorite dessert.

I make this all the time when I want to turn someone on to raw food. It takes only minutes to make, and it is incredibly good! I'm also going to give you my favorite appetizer; it's hard to believe it's not cooked!

Date Nut Torte

Fudgey, creamy and sweet!

Base of Torte:
2 cups raisins
2 cups walnuts

For Base:

1. In a food processor, combine raisins and walnuts and blend until well-blended and moist. (This will take a few minutes and you may see it forming a ball. Just make sure the raisins come out looking like a fudgey mixture and are not still grainy.)

2. Remove from processor and mold onto a plate in a round circle about 1½ inches thick.

Frosting:
1 cup dates, pitted and soaked
½ lemon, juiced

For Frosting:

1. In a food processor, combine dates and lemon juice until smooth and creamy.

2. Spread the frosting on top of the torte.

Note: I like this served at room temperature as the frosting and torte are still sticky, but if you want a firmer texture that will be easier to slice, refrigerate it for a few hours.

Pesto Stuffed Mushrooms

Served warm out of the dehydrator, these are heavenly! These taste like a soft, breaded, cooked, stuffed mushroom.

*18-24 button mushrooms, washed and
    stemmed*

Stuffing:
1 cup walnuts
½ cup pine nuts
2 cups basil
½ cup olive oil
3 cloves garlic
½ teaspoon sea salt

1. Place mushroom caps top side down on a plate.

2. Blend all stuffing ingredients in a food processor until smooth.

3. Scoop a small amount of stuffing into each mushroom cap.

4. Dehydrate at 105°F for 5–6 hours, or until soft.

Location: Massachusetts

Phone: 888-900-2529

Email: *alissa@alissacohen.com*

Website: *www.alissacohen.com*

Books: *Living on Live Food*

Alissa owned and operated her own health food establishment prior to becoming a full-time nutritional consultant.

Before (23 years old)

After (36 years old)

Gina S. Houston

Coming to the diet was most definitely Divine Intervention. I have been vegan for years, and it seems I kept hearing about how we are supposed to eat more raw fruits, vegetables, and nuts versus cooked foods for optimum health. People in my church would plant this information in my ear periodically. Then, one morning, I was listening to a radio show and they did a brief overview of the benefits of raw fooding. I knew it was God leading me to this lifestyle. I have been eating 80 percent raw and 20 percent cooked for about a year now, but I am officially 100 percent raw now.

My hair is much healthier and I hear constantly from women at my church that I am glowing. They ask me if I am in love and I laugh. I go places with other females that are in their 20s and people do not believe I am almost 40 years old.

I feel much more comfortable with the way I look now, and I am always asking God if He will let me look this way for the next twenty years. It is not arrogance at all, but I know that healthy inside does make you look healthy outside. True beauty comes from within first.

I wasn't beautiful growing up. I was always a chubby girl and I would always hear "You have such a pretty face, if you would just lose some of that weight." I felt like an ugly duckling because all of my cousins were thin and pretty, and I was an outcast at school.

Right now, I feel there are more hills to climb and higher heights. I am not on the level that other Raw-Foodist are and I want to go even more natural than my current status.

Creating a more natural environment for myself, such as living in a more spacious home with the capability to garden and have fruit trees. I believe I could live off the land literally and release this natural woman inside. Also, getting rid of emotional baggage that I have been toting for years. Being around those with a positive influence towards life.

I don't know about beauty secrets. I might be doing something that other women are doing every day. If I can say that I have one beauty secret, it is probably growing closer to God and realizing that He is as close as the air we breathe. I pay close attention to nature and recognize that you don't have to use a lot of chemicals on your skin to look your best.

I used to wear a ton of makeup, but all I have in my purse now is an all-natural tinted lip balm. That is it! I don't wear anything else. I wash with Shea Butter soap at night and smooth real Shea Butter over my face before going to sleep. I use natural toothpaste and organic skin creams and hair care products. There are a lot of chemicals and toxins in cosmetics that I believe affect our health in a negative way. I have endometriosis and having this ailment almost turns your body into a sponge. So I avoid makeup completely. I even buy unscented detergents and dry clean only as needed. We live in a toxic world, and it seems that the products made for women, such as cosmetics and makeup, are the most toxic.

My style is natural, but not extreme. Grooming is important to me. Some people think natural beauty is not tending to your hygiene and grooming needs, but that is not so. I am fortunate to have very low-maintenance hair and nails. My nails and hair have always been naturally long, so all I have to do is keep them groomed. I like native clothes, but fun stuff. I never got to wear jeans as a teenager, so now I wear them every weekend!

I used to wear nothing but black. I still have a lot of black in my wardrobe because it is very sensuous and is my signature color. But now I am wearing pastel colors. I used to never wear my hair down, but now I hardly ever have it pinned up. I am enjoying the freedom of being who I am because I feel closer to nature eating this way.

I desire to look and feel young for a long time. I have not yet had children and it is my desire to remain youthful so that no one will think they are my grandchildren when I start having them. I really do think going raw has made me look younger. Honestly, it feels great. Especially when college guys try to pick me up thinking I am their age and seriously do not believe me when I tell them my age. I have a 13-year-old nephew who is very mature, and, when I went to St. Louis last year, we sat together at church. A gentleman asked him if I was his girlfriend! Now *that* was cool!

Revealing my age depends on who is asking and why they are asking. I do not mind telling my age most of the time because I do not feel my age in my spirit. I have been told that my wisdom is the only thing that gives a clue to my age, because I do not look like I am in my late thirties.

I feel that people should be careful and tactful when asking a woman her age because it is a very private matter. Women are labeled hormonally and emotionally by society according to their age. When people find out I am 36 years old and I express my desire to have six children, I get all of these warnings on how my biological clock is ticking. Sharing my age is not a problem, but I do use discretion with certain people. Most of the time when I tell my age, I get more compliments than anything else, so it is almost always to my advantage to do so!

Guacamole

2 Pinkerton avocados (ripened)
14-16 organic spinach leaves
6 pieces sun-dried Roma tomatoes
(equivalent to
3 whole sun-dried tomatoes)
2-3 garlic cloves
juice of 1 large lime
1 teaspoon sea salt
1 teaspoon ground cumin

Peel the avocados and remove the pits. Reserve one pit for later use. Place all ingredients in a food processor using the "S" Blade. Pulse until all ingredients are well-blended and creamy. Transfer to a glass bowl and place the pit in the center of the guacamole. Chill for one hour. Serve with sliced zucchini squash and/or jicama.

Location: Tennessee

Gina is a dear friend and one of the raw food lifestyle's true success stories. She has culinary school experience and is very knowledgeable in the raw food preparation. Her sug-gestions on improving the recipe collection were invalu-able.

Recipes

"To eat is a necessity, but to eat intelligently is an art."

— La Rochefoucauld

Kitchen Equipment

The first step in the raw food diet is to make juicing a priority. If you are thinking about starting the raw food diet but do not want to make a heavy financial commitment, you can begin with the **standard blender,** found in almost every household. You can buy one at almost any drugstore or discount chain for $10-$20. Cheaper appliances can be more time consuming than the more expensive models, because the base ingredients may have to be cut in smaller pieces and fed into the blender slowly to achieve the full juicing effect. As you become more involved in the diet, you will probably want to upgrade to a more powerful blender like the **Vita-Mix.**

The next major investment will be a **juicer.** "Juicer" is something of a misnomer, because the average person automatically thinks about citrus juicers. In the raw food diet, however, fruit is usually eaten and the vegetables are turned into "juice." It is really closer to being pureed to a liquid form.

I have the **Champion Juicer,** which I highly recommend. In addition to your juicing needs, it can be used to create raw food recipes. The Champion is also a very durable machine and easy to clean. If you cannot invest in it immediately, get a less expensive juicer. My first juicer was very simple. It served me well for several years. While it is true that some juicers are better than others, the most important thing is to begin juicing as soon as possible, which is why I say that you can start with just a blender.

I was on the raw food diet for a whole year with only these two appliances.

When you are ready to move on from simply juicing, you will begin to add other appliances. In the raw food diet, one of the first steps after juicing is to start making daily salads that are slightly more complex than lettuce and tomatoes. There are two excellent additions to your raw kitchen that everyone should have even if they are not going raw. First is the **spiral slicer (saladacco)** which is a very useful gadget for the raw food lifestyle. Some health food stores carry this wonderful device, or you can buy it online. Search the internet for the best price available.

A saladacco is great for making live pasta. By setting the blade to the desired width and simply rotating the handle, you can make long ribbons and thin strands from firm, whole vegetables like carrots, squash, radishes and zucchini. A clear plastic base collects the vegetable cuttings. After you've finished cutting, at least 1-inch of leftover vegetable is left. No problem! Use it in your next juice.

The second is the **mandoline slicer** which is great for making salads. It cuts professional-looking, same-size slices from all kinds of vegetables and considerably decreases salad preparation time. I use a very simple hand-held model. It has a double-edged blade to slice in a back and forth motion. Numerous models are available; some models have protective holders. Check your local cookware store or search the internet for the best model and price for your needs.

When you are ready to start preparing more complicated dishes, it's time for a **food processor.** I was delighted to learn about the versatility of this appliance. It comes with several blades to let you quickly shred, grate, and slice. I suggest buying a food processor as the next major step. **Cuisinart** is the best, but a $30 processor from Wal-Mart will get you started. If you are only preparing meals for yourself, it is possible to get by with mini-processors for a while.

Food processors are perfect for making crusts, date paste, and pâtés, and for grating cabbage and other vegetables. They make raw food preparation a lot easier, and they work with dry ingredients where a blender cannot. If you need a cheap way to work with dry ingredients before you invest in a processor, a **coffee grinder** will work. Again, it is more labor-intensive and time-consuming, but it will achieve the necessary results.

SPROUTING

One of things that makes the raw food diet special is its emphasis on using fresh sprouts. Anyone who grew up in a rural, crop-oriented environment knows the basics of sprouting seeds. It was the first thing you did in the spring to establish the fertility count of the crop seeds so the planter could be set to compensate, thus ensuring the best possible yield. The principle is the same on the raw food diet, except that you eat the sprouts.

While there are many methods for sprouting that you can investigate, I use the jar method. To start sprouting, use a clean glass jar of about 8-10 ounces. You can recycle any wide-mouthed jar you may have on hand, or purchase a wide-mouthed glass canning jar. You will have to cut a lid from plastic mesh screen and attach it with a rubber band, or purchase lids designed for sprouting.

Be sure your seeds are fresh. Look them over carefully to be sure that they are clean. This is no different than checking berries for stems, etc. My rule of thumb is that the seeds basically double when sprouted, so one cup of seeds will produce two cups of sprouts.

After you have rinsed the seeds, place them in the jar, fill it with water and let them soak. I usually soak seeds overnight, although the length of time may vary according to the seeds. You will quickly discern any differences that suit your individual preferences. After soaking, drain off the water and re-rinse the seeds. Prop the jar at a 45 degree angle, with the opening down to continue drainage.

Keep the seeds out of direct sunlight, rinsing them several times a day and always replacing the jar at a downward angle. Continue rinsing the sprouts daily as long as you are using them. They may be kept in the refrigerator, but they should be eaten as soon as possible because freshness is crucial.

Juices

The ingredients must be fresh to be full of wholesome live energy. Juice cannot be prepared in advance because it will lose its healing properties. Fresh juice must be drunk immediately. After only 15 minutes, fresh produce drastically loses its vital qualities. When you start juicing you may dilute your first juices with water.

Beginner's Blood-Building Juice

*2 medium **apples***
3 medium carrots
*½ small **beet root***

Juice all ingredients and drink immediately.

APPLES

Apples really do help keep the doctor away. With most fiber being the insoluble type known as roughage, apples are a good source of pectin, a soluble fiber (a medium apple has 4 grams). Soluble fiber dissolves in water and becomes gummy. It lowers cholesterol, aids in appetite control, and immensely improves digestion. Pectin reduces cholesterol and helps maintain steady blood sugar levels.

Apples are rich in vitamins A, B_1, B_2, B_6, biotin, folic acid, and pantothenic acid. They also have high mineral content, which makes them beneficial for the health of your skin, hair, and fingernails.

You should never peel apples. Apple skin is a source of quercetin, an antioxidant that keeps the heart and lungs healthy. An English study of more than 2,600 people found that people who eat an apple daily have better lung capacity than those who don't eat apples as frequently. *I can attest to the results. I have been eating an apple every single day for years and my lung capacity recently tested amazingly high.*

The English study also found that eating apples may reduce the risk of lung cancer while boosting resistance to respiratory illnesses. "Apples contain a huge number of protective compounds called flavonoids, which are absorbed by the body and help make lung tissue healthier and more resistant to disease," explains John Britton, M.D., who conducted the study.

This juice is delicious and very energizing. It will help you become accustomed to drinking freshly made juices regularly.

Eyesight Enhancer

*3 medium **carrots***
3 celery stalks
2 medium apples

Juice all ingredients and drink immediately.

CARROTS

The word "carrot" is related to the ancient Greek word *karoten*. Carrot juice was commonly used in ancient Greece to cure stomach disorders of all kinds.

Carrots improve a variety of digestive problems. The three most important elements in carrots are beta-carotene, vitamin A, and phytochemicals. With these three elements, carrots improve muscle, soft tissue, and skin health; reduce the risk of heart disease and high blood pressure, boost immunity (especially among older people), and protect the skin from sun damage.

Carrots are also highly effective in the treatment of complexion problems — specifically acne, boils, cysts, and rough and dry skin. The potassium that is prevalent in carrot juice neutralizes excess acid and releases vitamin A.

Carrot juice is highly beneficial for vision problems. For anyone suffering eyestrain, occasional blurred vision, or problems with night vision, carrots may be the perfect food.

With all this said, carrot juice may give some people's skin an orange hue; however, it will not affect others. This pigment change usually happens if you drink more than five glasses of straight carrot juice per week. It is a sign that the liver is excreting a great amount of toxins. If this occurs, decrease the amount of carrots in your juice and the condition will reverse itself within a week or two.

Eye Bag Remover

*1 small **beet** (beet root and beet greens)*
3 celery stalks
2 medium apples
½ small organic lemon with the skin

Juice all ingredients and drink immediately.

BEET ROOTS AND BEET GREENS

Beets are a common root vegetable that is delicious raw. They are colorful and make an excellent decorative element in raw creations.

Beet greens contain an abundance of chlorophyll and vitamins A and C. It is also has a high mineral content, being especially rich in calcium and potassium.

Beet juice can be combined with green juices. Beets contain fiber and vitamins C and K. They are also rich in folate, a natural substance which aids in preventing certain birth defects, and heart disease. The betaine in beet juice is said to stimulate the function of liver cells and protect the liver and bile ducts.

Including beet root and beet greens in your juice is an excellent way to detoxify the blood and renew it with minerals and natural sugars. These elements help reconstitute the blood, bringing important sustenance to the brain, heart, lungs, liver, and kidneys — including those weakened by alcohol and other drugs.

Including beet root in your juice helps to alleviate menstrual disturbances and menopausal symptoms.

When buying beets, look for healthy, firm, wrinkle-free ones. Beets, being root vegetables, keep a long time. Beet greens must be used in a juice within a couple of days.

I include one small or medium beet root in almost all of my juices. I believe that I do not have bags under my eyes because this amazing root is a powerful kidney and blood cleanser.

Bone Strengthener

3 medium zucchini
2 celery stalks
1 small beet root
2 medium apples

Juice all ingredients and drink immediately.

ZUCCHINI

Today's squash is descended from a wild squash that was originally found between Guatemala and Mexico. The first squash, which goes back over 10,000 years, was nearly inedible and was cultivated primarily for its seeds. Gradually, varieties with abundant, sweet-tasting flesh were developed. Christopher Columbus introduced squash to Europe. Like many of the foods from the New World, its cultivation spread throughout Spain and Portugal.

Zucchini is the best-known of the summer squash. It is narrow and elongated, resembling a cucumber in size and shape. It has smooth, thin, green or yellow skin which may be striped or speckled. The edible blossoms are used in salads and as garnishes. It is related to melons as well as cucumbers.

Zucchini is an excellent source of potassium and magnesium, which are beneficial to those people taking diuretics for high blood pressure because the medication can leach these minerals from the body. Zucchini juice helps strengthen bones and prevents brittleness because the chelated calcium content is so high that it is retained by the body longer than calcium from dairy or food supplements. In zucchini, the calcium, phosphorus, magnesium, and sodium amounts are fairly equally balanced. The high potassium count, combined with the other contents, helps bones mend faster.

Zucchini is another ingredient I use in almost all of my juices. It gives a mild taste to the juice. It worked wonders for me after my hip surgery. My bones healed very quickly.

Complexion Clarifier

*4 pickle-size **cucumbers***
3 stalks of celery
2 medium carrots
2 medium apples

Juice all ingredients and drink immediately.

CUCUMBERS

Cucumbers belong to the same family as pumpkin, zucchini, watermelon, and other types of squash.

The silica in cucumber is an essential component of healthy connective tissue, which includes intracellular cement, muscles, tendons, ligaments, cartilage, and bone.

Cucumber juice is often recommended as a source of silicon to improve the complexion and health of the skin; plus, cucumber's high water content makes it naturally hydrating — a must for glowing skin.

Paul Bragg said this about cucumber juice: "there is nothing more nourishing for the skin to have than the liquid juice from the cucumber. The nutrition-rich water that it contains, when taken into the body, adds luster to the hair, sparkle to the eye, color to the lips, tone to the skin, and spring to the step."

It is said that Mr. Bragg didn't have many wrinkles although he spent a lot of time in the sun because cucumber juice was a daily part of his diet.

Some think that the natural oils present in the peel may have something to do with how resilient and remarkably clear the skin can look following a lengthy period of cucumber juicing. And there is the added bonus of vitamin C, silica, potassium, and magnesium.

I always use cucumbers in my juice when they are in season. Nothing else comes close to their ability to improve the complexion!

Scarlet Beauty Juice

*5 medium **tomatoes***
2 medium carrots
1 medium beet root

Juice all ingredients and drink immediately.

TOMATOES

Tomatoes are a native American plant originally grown by the Aztecs and Incas for hundreds of years. The Conquistadors introduced the plant to Europe, where it became an essential ingredient in Mediterranean cooking. The British, however, considered it poisonous (it does belong to the deadly nightshade family) and did not include it in their diet. It was introduced into American cuisine in the early 19th century by the Creoles.

Tomatoes are actually a fruit because, botanically, the edible part contains the seeds.

In the nutrition field, nothing has been hotter in the last five years than studies on the lycopene in tomatoes. This carotenoid nutrient has been extensively studied for its antioxidant and cancer-preventing properties

Tomatoes are also an excellent source of biotin, a B-vitamin involved in the metabolism of both sugar and fat. A cup of fresh tomato will give you 24 percent of the daily value of biotin, so eating tomatoes can help improve energy production, skin health, and nervous system function.

Tomatoes also contain vitamin K. The 17.1 percent of the daily value for vitamin K that is found in one cup of raw tomato is important for maintaining bone health. Vitamin K_1 activates osteocalcin, the major non-collagen protein in bone. Without enough vitamin K_1, osteocalcin levels are inadequate, and bone mineralization is impaired.

In addition, tomatoes are a very good source of riboflavin, which has been shown to be helpful for reducing the frequency of migraine attacks in those who suffer from them.

Try to find local farmers who grow organic tomatoes. During its season, the taste of these tomatoes will be infinitely superior to the ones sold in the supermarkets.

Health Enhancing Juice

2 medium **parsnips**
3 medium carrots
2 stalks celery
2 medium apples
¼ inch ginger root

Juice all ingredients and drink immediately.

PARSNIPS

This cream-colored member of the carrot family traces its fat roots back to Eastern Europe and the Mediterranean region. In many countries of Europe, like Holland and my native Russia, parsnips are used in soups. In Ireland, cottagers make a type of beer by boiling the roots with water and hops.

Parsnips have a tough, wiry root, tapering somewhat at the crown. An erect stem, one to two feet high, tough and furrowed, grows from the top.

A strong dose of the root is a good diuretic and assists in removing obstructions of the viscera. It has been used to treat stomach ailments, jaundice, and kidney stones.

John Wesley, in his *Primitive Physic,* says: "Wild parsnips both leaves and stalks, bruised, seem to have been a favorite application; and a very popular internal remedy for cancer, asthma, consumption and similar diseases."

Parsnip roots are sweeter than carrots. They contain both sugar and starch, which makes for a tasty drink. The roots can be peeled but are more nutritious if the skin is simply brushed thoroughly under cold water.

According to John Heinerman in *Heinerman's Encyclopedia of Healing Juices,* parsnips are "working wonders" for hair, skin, and nails.

Parsnips are usually sold side by side with carrots in every grocery store.

Ruby Rejuvenating Juice

*4 stalks **celery***
3 medium carrots
1 medium beet root
1 medium apple
½ lemon with the skin

Juice all ingredients and drink immediately.

CELERY

Chinese medical practitioners have used celery's beneficial blood-pressure-reducing action for a long time. Now scientists have discovered what makes it work.

Celery contains active compounds called phthalides, which relax the muscles of the arteries that regulate blood pressure, allowing these vessels to dilate. Phthalides also reduce stress hormones, the effect of one of which is to cause blood vessels to constrict.

Including four stalks of celery in your morning juice can lower high blood pressure by 12 to 14 percent.

Celery also contains compounds called coumarins that help prevent free radicals from damaging cells, thus decreasing the mutations that increase the potential for cells to become cancerous. Coumarin magnifies the activity of certain white blood cells, immune defenders that target and eliminate potentially harmful cells, including cancer cells. In addition, compounds in celery called acetylenics have been shown to stop the growth of tumor cells.

As the raw food diet is very low in sodium, it is crucial that celery, which is high in organic sodium, be included in your daily juice. Celery, along with an apple, is a constant ingredient in my morning juice.

Invigorating Emerald Juice

*1 stem of **broccoli***
3 stalks celery
3 cucumbers
2 medium Granny Smith apples

Juice all ingredients and drink immediately.

BROCCOLI

Four ounces of raw broccoli contains about 100 milligrams of vitamin C. Very fresh broccoli, which has a bluish-green hue, can contain up to 40 percent more. Because vitamin C is the main antioxidant in blood, some researchers suggest that it may help protect against atherosclerotic deposits.

Sulforaphane, a chemical contained in most varieties of broccoli, has been shown to kill the *Helicobacter pylori* bacterium widely considered responsible for most cases of peptic ulcers and gastritis. It also protects human retinal cells from damage that can cause blindness through cataracts or macular degeneration.

Broccoli is an excellent source of fiber, vitamins C and K, beta-carotene, and folate (a B-vitamin that is important in reducing the risk of birth defects).

Recent studies by the FDA have shown that freezing, boiling, blanching, steaming, or otherwise cooking broccoli depletes its nutrients exponentially. Steaming does the least damage, but, obviously, raw is the winner with no loss at all. A half-cup daily is the recommended amount.

I use broccoli stems for juicing and use the florets in salads.

Anti-Aging Asparagus Juice

*8 **asparagus** spears*
3 small zucchini squash
3 stalks celery
2 medium sweet apples

Juice all ingredients and drink immediately.

ASPARAGUS

Asparagus was used as a medicine long before it was eaten as a vegetable. It contains a substance called *asparagines,* an effective diuretic which breaks up oxalic and uric acid crystals in the kidneys and muscles, eliminating them through the urine. Asparagine is also responsible for the strong odor often produced in the urine after eating asparagus — a harmless and temporary side effect.

The green tips of asparagus are particularly rich in glutathione, an antioxidant protein that functions in the body as a detoxifying agent, a defender against certain cancers and viruses, as well as an immune cell booster.

Pregnant women should make asparagus a frequent addition to their meals. A cup of asparagus supplies approximately 263 mcg of folate, a B-vitamin essential for proper cellular division because it is necessary in DNA synthesis.

Without folate, the fetus's nervous system cells do not divide properly. Inadequate folate during pregnancy has been linked to several birth defects, including neural tube defects like spina bifida.

Asparagus is high in potassium and low in sodium. Traditionally, asparagus has been used to treat problems involving swelling, such as arthritis and rheumatism, and may also be useful for PMS-related water retention.

Asparagus is rich in folic acid, vitamin E, and beta-carotene. It is an excellent source of selenium, a powerful anti-acid microelement. This mineral is an essential anti-aging element, especially for the skin, which it helps to keep supple.

Salads &
Dressings

Basic Salad

*1 cup **baby (spring) greens***
1 cup tomatoes, cut in cubes
1 cup cucumbers, cut in cubes
½ avocado, cut in cubes
2 green onions, minced
sea salt to taste
2 tablespoons olive oil
1 tablespoon lemon juice

To make the salad: Place baby greens on a large plate or a small serving platter. Layer remaining ingredients on top of baby greens and serve.

BABY GREENS

Baby greens are any combination of young greens: lettuce, spinach, arugula, chard, kale, and others. Baby greens are the very young leaves of the plants. Their dimensions are usually only about 1 to 1½ inches in length. The young leaves are more tender and milder than the adult plants, and they are bite-sized.

Spring greens, as they are sometimes called, contain all of the healthy vitamins and minerals found in the mature plants. They are chock full of vitamins A and B as well as minerals such as zinc, calcium, niacin, and iron. All of these help in the fight against bone loss, high blood pressure, diabetes, high cholesterol, hypertension, heart attack, and cancer just like the fully grown greens.

Baby greens can be purchased in the produce section already bagged in several varieties to suit the individual taste.

New Millennium Salad

2 cups baby greens
*1 cup **jicama**, shredded or spiralized*
1 cup butternut squash, shredded or
  spiralized
1 cup zucchini, shredded or spiralized
1 pint cherry tomatoes

Place all the shredded (or spiralized) ingredients on top of the baby greens. Arrange the cherry tomatoes on the plate in a decorative way. You can serve this salad with Tropical Dressing.

JICAMA

The jicama plant, also called yam bean or Mexican turnip, originated in Mexico. It is a legume and is grown for its large tuberous roots, which can be eaten raw or cooked. The plant is a vine which grows to a length of 20 feet or more. The roots are light brown in color, and may weigh up to 50 pounds. Most of those at the market weigh between three and five pounds.

They must be peeled but may then be eaten raw or cooked. Sliced, the jicama can be used like potato chips with dip. Jicama is crunchy, juicy, a little sweet, and not as starchy as a potato. Raw jicama is very crisp, with an apple-like, nutty flavor.

The jicama is abundant in fiber, potassium, iron, calcium, and vitamin A, B-complex, and C. It is low in calories and saturated fats and is sodium-free. Its combination of vitamins and minerals has been proven to reduce cancer risk and coronary heart disease by decreasing fat and cholesterol. Decreased sodium intake can reduce hypertension.

You can buy jicama in every health food store, some grocery stores, and in Wal-Mart.

Lettuce, Kohlrabi & Currant Salad

1 head romaine lettuce, chopped
*1 small **kohlrabi**, shredded*
½ cup dried currants
½ cup macadamia cheese
½ red bell pepper, sliced
1 tablespoon olive oil
1 tablespoon lemon juice
sea salt to taste

In a salad bowl, combine chopped lettuce and shredded kohlrabi. Layer dried currants and clumps of macadamia cheese on top of lettuce and kohlrabi. In a separate small bowl, combine olive oil, lemon juice, and sea salt, and toss with vegetables. Garnish with sliced red bell pepper.

KOHLRABI

Kohlrabi is referenced as far back as the first century A.D., when Pliny the Elder called it a Corinthian turnip. It appears in the world's first known cookbook by Apicius from Imperial Rome.

Kohlrabi, however, is no longer a popular vegetable. While still widely available, it is likely to be greeted with bewilderment because so few people recognize it. A member of the cabbage family, its base looks like a turnip but grows above ground. Kohlrabi is German for cabbage turnip.

Kohlrabi's flavor is much milder than its kinfolk — broccoli and cauliflower — but it does have hints of both. Its texture is crisp and moist. Kohlrabi traditionally comes in two varieties, purple and green. The purple is considered the sweeter. Both have pale green flesh inside. Ideally, they should be small (1½-2 inches) for the best flavor. The smaller ones do not need to be peeled.

Like most vegetables, kohlrabi is low in calories (19 per ½ cup raw) and high in dietary fiber (2.5 grams per ½ cup). It contains potassium, vitamin A, vitamin C, folic acid, and calcium in high enough quantities to be beneficial.

I find it absolutely delicious in salads.

Whole Turnip Salad

*1 cup **turnip greens**, chopped*
sea salt to taste
olive oil
juice of ½ lemon
*1 medium **turnip** root, spiralized*
1 medium zucchini, spiralized
½ avocado, sliced

Toss greens with sea salt, olive oil, and lemon juice. Grind ingredients with a wooden spoon or pestle. Add turnip root, zucchini, and avocado. Mix well. Serve immediately.

TURNIPS/TURNIP GREENS

Turnip greens are far more likely to be eaten than turnips themselves, especially in the Southern states.

Both turnip greens and turnip roots are supercharged with so many different nutrients that their consumption can help prevent or heal a wide range of health conditions.

They are an excellent source of beta-carotene, vitamin C, vitamin E, vitamin B_6, folate, copper, calcium, and dietary fiber.

An excellent source of the mineral copper, turnip greens may help those with rheumatoid arthritis, as copper is necessary for the production of connective tissue, which is damaged in this autoimmune condition. Since rheumatoid arthritis can cause bone loss — thus increasing the risk of osteoporosis — the calcium provided is also of special benefit.

Turnips boast significant amounts of a healthy antioxidant combination: vitamin C, vitamin E, and beta-carotene. The vitamin C and vitamin E work in concert to quench free radicals that can otherwise exacerbate joint damage.

Studies have shown that people with the greatest intake of vitamin E have approximately one-third the risk of developing colon cancer compared to those with the lowest intake of this fat-soluble antioxidant.

Beta-carotene, a powerful antioxidant in its own right, can be converted by the body into vitamin A, which has been shown to decrease the risks of developing both colon and rectal cancer.

Napa Cabbage Cole Slaw

1 cup shredded **napa cabbage**
¼ medium red onion, diced
½ green bell pepper, chopped
½ cup shredded Granny Smith apples
¼ cup chopped fresh dill
2 tablespoons olive oil
juice of ½ medium lemon
sea salt to taste

In a large salad bowl, combine all ingredients. Toss until well coated. Allow to stand 15 minutes and serve. Will keep refrigerated 1–2 days.

NAPA CABBAGE

While several types of Chinese cabbage exist, the variety we most commonly associate with Chinese cabbage is napa cabbage, the large-headed cabbage with the firmly packed, pale green leaves that you'll usually find next to bok choy in western supermarkets.

Napa cabbage has long, oblong-shaped leaves that are flat and wide. They are pale green, fading towards greenish white in the center. Napa cabbage resembles a head of compact Romaine lettuce with curly edges. It has a mild sweet flavor similar to a combination of cabbage, iceberg lettuce, and celery.

Healthier than western cabbages, napa cabbage is rich in vitamin C and other nutrients. It is fat free, cholesterol free, and low in sodium and calories. All of these characteristics are known to reduce the risks of cancer, coronary heart disease, and hypertension.

Look for firm green leaves that are not wilted. Store in a plastic bag in the crisper section. Like tofu, napa cabbage absorbs the flavors of the foods around it. It should be eaten immediately because it begins to lose its vitamin C content as soon as it is cut.

*The dressings featured in this section may be used with any salad in which olive oil, lemon juice, or sea salt are **not** used. You can also try them on salads of your own creation.*

Avocado-Lemon Dressing

1 **avocado,** pitted and peeled
2 tablespoons raw tahini
2 cloves garlic, minced
3 tablespoons lemon juice
¼ inch ginger root
coconut water, as needed
sea salt to taste
water as needed
1 tablespoon parsley, minced

Combine all ingredients except parsley in a blender or Vita-Mix. Blend until mixture is creamy. Stir in parsley and use on your favorite salad.

AVOCADO

The avocado is a great source of monounsaturated fat (known to keep cholesterol levels down). Recent research from California growers has shown that the variety of avocado called "Haas" is one of the best.

Avocados have nearly twice as much vitamin E as previously thought, making them the highest fruit source for this powerful antioxidant. Antioxidants help the body by absorbing free radicals that are known to cause increased risk in the development of heart disease and some cancers.

Glutathione, a phytochemical found in fruits and vegetables, acts as an antioxidant. For absorbing free radicals, avocado contains three times the glutathione (an antioxidant) of other leading fruits. Because they are a good source of glutathione, avocados may offer some protection against oral, throat, and other types of cancer.

Avocados are the highest fruit source of lutein, which protects against cataracts and macular degeneration. Recent research finds that avocados pack more cholesterol-smashing beta-sitosterol than any other fruit

Beta-sitosterol is an important phytosterol. High phytosterol intake has been linked with lower blood cholesterol levels. Among all commonly eaten fruits, oranges and avocados contain the most beta-sitosterol and contain at least twice the amount of the phytosterol found in other foods, including corn, green soybeans, and olives.

Tahini Salad Dressing

3 tablespoons raw **tahini**
1 coconut (meat and water)
2 cloves garlic
juice of 1 small lemon
sea salt to taste

Combine all ingredients in a blender and blend well. Store in a clear jar or container. This dressing will keep in the refrigerator for 2 or 3 days.

TAHINI/SESAME SEEDS

Tahini, a healthy alternative to butter, is a spread made from sesame seeds.

Sesame seeds have been used for thousands of years. Raw sesame seeds, with their husks intact, are darkish-brown in color, compared with the more common dehulled white seeds. Ancient Arabs used them as food for traveling long distances.

Sesame seeds are 19 percent protein and an excellent source of B vitamins and minerals. They are considered one of the highest sources of calcium in the world when the husk is intact.

The white to lavender-pink flowers mature into seed-containing pods which burst with a pop when mature. This scatters the seeds, so the pods must be harvested by hand before they are fully ripe. Sesame seed hulls are often removed because they contain 2 to 3 percent oxalic acid, which has a bitter flavor and can interfere with the absorption of calcium.

Although sesame seeds contain no cholesterol, they are still 50 percent unsaturated fat, so those watching their fat consumption should exercise moderation. Fortunately, a small amount goes a long way in flavoring foods.

Sesame seeds have a high magnesium content, which helps to steady the nerves; they are also used in laxatives as an emollient. Some studies show that *sesamin,* a lignin found only in sesame seeds, has remarkable antioxidant effects, which can inhibit the absorption of cholesterol as well as the production of cholesterol in the liver.

The seeds are also rich in vitamins A and E and protein. Sesame seeds are a very good source of the minerals copper, magnesium, and calcium. Tahini is sold in health food stores. Be sure that the label says RAW. *Because of its high calcium content, I try to use it often in my dressings and desserts. It is a pleasure, since it is so delicious.*

Tropical Dressing

1 cup pineapple, cubed
1 cup mango, sliced
1 cup papaya, sliced
*⅓ inch **ginger root***
juice of 1 small lemon
sea salt to taste

In a blender or Vita-Mix, combine all ingredients and mix until smooth. Serve immediately on salad of your choice.

GINGER ROOT

First cultivated by the Chinese, ginger's origins are uncertain, because it has never been found in the wild. Its name is thought to come from Sanskrit *sinabera,* meaning "shaped like an antler." Ginger is the underground stem of the plant.

It became one of the major spices responsible for the spice routes to the Orient. It is said that during the Middle Ages, a pound of ginger was equivalent in worth to a full-grown sheep.

Ginger is most commonly called after its place of origin: Jamaican, African, or Cochin. It has been used for centuries, not just as flavoring, but also for medicinal purposes.

Ginger increases circulation and reduces the pain of osteoarthritis. You can often reduce arthritis or bursitis pain with a ginger bath. Because it acts as an antihistamine, ginger is ideal for anyone with a cold. Ginger also stimulates the immune system and lowers fevers by stimulating perspiration.

A small piece of ginger after a meal will aid digestion and reduce gas. It also works for seasickness. Ginger improves blood flow and creates a warm sensation throughout the body, which can stimulate sexual activity.

Ginger can be found in the produce section. Wal-Mart usually has the lowest price for the root.

When transitioning to the raw food diet, many people feel like their feet and hands are getting cold. Adding ginger to your meals and juices will improve circulation and will give a warming sensation.

Papaya Tomato Dressing

*1 cup ripe **papaya**, cut in chunks*
1 cup fresh tomatoes, chopped
1 tablespoon fresh basil, chopped
2 tablespoons olive oil
juice of ½ medium lemon
¼ inch ginger root
sea salt to taste
water as needed
1 tablespoon fresh parsley, chopped

Mix all ingredients except parsley in a blender or Vita-Mix. Stir in parsley and serve on a salad of your choice.

PAPAYA

Papayas are native to Central America. It is said that Christopher Columbus called it "the fruit of the angels." The New World explorers took papayas to other subtropical climates, including India and Africa.

Papayas offer the luscious taste and sunlit color of their homelands, and are rich sources of antioxidant nutrients such as carotenes, vitamin C, flavonoids, B vitamins, folate, and pantothenic acid, the minerals potassium and magnesium, and fiber. Together, these nutrients promote the health of the cardiovascular system and provide protection against colon cancer.

Papayas are also a very good source of fiber, which has been shown to lower high cholesterol levels. The nutrients in papaya have been shown to be helpful in the prevention of colon cancer. Papaya's fiber is able to bind to cancer-causing toxins in the colon and keep them away from healthy colon cells. In addition, papaya's folate, vitamin C, beta-carotene, and vitamin E have each been associated with a reduced risk of colon cancer.

The fiber found in papayas may also help with the symptoms of those suffering from irritable bowel syndrome. In addition, vitamin C and vitamin A, which is made in the body from the beta-carotene in papaya, are both needed for the proper function of a healthy immune system.

Delicious Dulse Dressing

*⅓ cup **dulse** strips, soaked for 10-15*
*   minutes*
½ cup pine nuts, soaked for several hours
¼ small beet (to add color)
½ cup sun-dried tomatoes,
*   soaked overnight*
1 tablespoon dill, chopped
⅛ teaspoon cayenne pepper
1 tablespoon raw honey
1 clove garlic
sea salt to taste

Place all ingredients in a blender or Vita-Mix. Blend on high until smooth. Serve on basic salad.

DULSE

Dulse is reddish in color with a soft, chewy texture. It has a salty, spicy flavor that makes it a good introduction to sea vegetables.

Dulse is a rich, natural source of essential nutrients. Full of minerals like titanium and iodine, with an assortment of vitamins and essential amino acids, dulse has few calories and no cholesterol or fat, and it is already seasoned by natural sea salt.

Dulse is a source of potassium, an essential cellular ion. A recent study suggests that most Westerners have a potassium deficiency, because their cooking method leaches essential potassium out of vegetables. It is thrown out with the cooking water. Eating dulse is an excellent way of obtaining potassium in the diet.

Dulse can also prevent seasickness, inhibits the herpes virus *(in vitro),* and, because of its high iron content, is excellent for those with anemia. It is also a rich source of trace minerals.

Seaweed consumption is essential because of the low sodium content of the rawsome diet. It is good source of protein, iron, chlorophyll, iodine, potassium, and active enzymes.

Its salty taste reduces or eliminates need for salt. Dulse gives this dressing a unique seafood flavor.

You can buy dry dulse in health food stores.

Living Soups

Savory Parsnip Soup

2 medium parsnips, scraped and
    cut in chunks
¼ head cauliflower, cut in chunks
1 tablespoon lemon juice
1 tablespoon olive oil
½ teaspoon cumin
½ teaspoon cayenne pepper
sea salt to taste
2 cups water
½ cup chopped sweet **onion**
½ cup red bell pepper, diced
¼ cup pine nuts, soaked overnight

Combine parsnips, cauliflower, lemon juice, oil, cumin, cayenne pepper, sea salt, and water in a blender or Vita-Mix. Blend until a smooth, creamy mixture is produced. Pour the mixture into a bowl. Stir in diced onion and red bell pepper. Garnish with pepper strips and pine nuts before serving.

ONION

As both Sanskrit and Hebrew literature show, onions have been cultivated longer than most vegetables. Onions, like garlic, are members of the *Allium* family, and both are rich in powerful sulfur-containing compounds that are responsible for their pungent odors and for many of their health-promoting effects.

Onions possess antibiotic-like qualities and act as a diuretic, blood pressure regulator, and antiseptic. Onions can also be helpful getting rid of intestinal parasites.

Onions may help prevent ulcers by prohibiting growth of the ulcer-causing bacteria. Onions are very rich in chromium, a trace mineral that helps cells respond to insulin; they are also high in vitamin C and numerous flavonoids.

The higher the intake of onion, the lower the level of glucose found during oral or intravenous glucose tolerance tests. Allyl propyl disulfide is responsible for this. It competes with insulin, which is also a disulfide, to occupy the sites in the liver where insulin is deactivated. This results in an increase in the amount of insulin available to usher glucose into cells, causing a lowering of blood sugar.

Chilled Cucumber Soup

3 marinated cucumbers
1 cup apple cider vinegar
1 cup water (for marinating cucumbers)
½ cup pumpkin seeds, soaked overnight
1 tablespoon lemon juice
*2 cloves **garlic**, minced*
pinch cayenne pepper
sea salt to taste
3 cups water
1 tablespoon fresh dill

To marinate cucumbers: Slice cucumbers. Place cucumbers in a medium-size container, and add 1 cup apple cider vinegar and 1 cup water. Allow to marinate on counter for 2 days.

To prepare soup: Combine pumpkin seeds, lemon juice, garlic, cayenne pepper, sea salt, and 3 cups water in a blender or Vita-Mix. Blend until smooth and creamy. Pour the mixture into a bowl. Chop marinated cucumber slices and add to mixture. Discard the marinade. Garnish with fresh dill. Chill before serving.

GARLIC

Garlic goes back to ancient Greece, Egypt, and the time of Moses. Like so many other fruits and vegetables in our normal diet, garlic also appeared in ancient Rome, where it was said to be used to clear the arteries. It was used from Roman times until after World War I as a poultice to reduce the possibility of infections. Some of Louis Pasteur's early experiments used garlic to kill bacteria. Garlic was called "Russian penicillin" during World War II because the Russians used it for treating the military after the antibiotic supply was depleted.

Studies have found that daily garlic supplements reduce one's risk of catching a cold by half. The same study found that those who caught colds while using garlic recovered more quickly.

Garlic and onions are both considered highly beneficial in the prevention and treatment of stomach cancer. A study done in a Chinese province with a high rate of stomach cancer showed that those who ate significantly more garlic did not have cancer. More extensive research is needed, but it appears that garlic may protect against stomach cancer by its ability to decrease gastritis.

Regularly eating garlic lowers blood pressure. In other beneficial actions, garlic helps prevent atherosclerosis and diabetic heart disease, and reduces the risk of heart attack or stroke. Two or more servings of garlic a week may help protect against colon cancer.

I recommend using fresh garlic as often as you can.

Cauliflower Cream Soup

2 cups **cauliflower**, *chopped in chunks*
1 medium avocado
½ cup sunflower seeds, soaked overnight
1 tablespoon raw honey
2 tablespoons lemon juice
sea salt to taste
2 cups water
2 tablespoons fresh dill, chopped

Blend all ingredients except dill in a blender or Vita-Mix. Garnish with dill before serving.

CAULIFLOWER

The cauliflower, a crucifer, is related to the cabbage. The cruciferous family includes broccoli, cabbage, kale, and Brussels sprouts. Cauliflower can be chopped into salads or used to dip in pâtés and guacamole.

Cauliflower is rich in calcium, boron, iron, and other minerals. It is reputed to have cancer-fighting nutrients in the form of antioxidants. These compounds appear to stop enzymes from activating cancer-causing agents in the body, and they increase the activity of enzymes that disable and eliminate carcinogens.

Many enzymes found in cauliflower also help with the detoxifying process. Both animal and human studies show increased detoxification enzyme levels from high glucosinolate diets. Researchers suggest that a high intake of cruciferous vegetables helps decrease the risk of certain cancers.

Collard Greens Mushroom Soup

1 cup buckwheat, soaked and sprouted
2 cups mushrooms
2 strips of kelp, cup into small pieces
*2 leaves of **collard greens,***
  cut in tiny, short strips
1 parsnip, shredded
1 carrot, shredded
2 cups Nama Shoyu
2 cups water
2 tablespoons lemon juice
½ cup scallions, minced
1 tablespoon olive oil

Soak 1 cup of buckwheat overnight and then sprout for 2 days.

Marinate mushrooms, kelp, collard greens, parsnip, and carrot in a mixture of Nama Shoyu, water, lemon juice, and olive oil in a large glass bowl overnight. Store in refrigerator. Discard marinade. Add buckwheat, water, and scallions to the marinated mixture. Remove all trays from the dehydrator. Place the bowl inside the dehydrator and keep it running at 108°F, warming the soup for several hours before serving.

COLLARD GREENS

Collard greens (also known as tree-cabbage or non-heading cabbage) have a very mild, almost smoky flavor. Their dark blue-green, smooth leaves differentiate them from the frilly-edged kale. They like cool weather and are best from January through April. They are a staple in Southern diets but are not as popular in other regions.

As members of the *Brassica* genus of foods, collards stand out as an anti-cancer food. Ten to fifteen glucosinolates are present in collards; glucosinolates appear to be able to lessen the occurrence of a wide variety of cancers, including breast and ovarian cancers.

Collard greens are a very good source of calcium, which helps maintain bone strength and density. Recent studies have shown that calcium also helps protect colon cells from cancer-causing chemicals, as well as preventing bone loss from menopause or rheumatoid arthritis. It also helps prevent migraine headaches and reduces PMS symptoms.

Collard greens are an excellent source of vitamin A and a good source of zinc — both nutrients that help immune system function. Collards help reduce the risk of cardiovascular disease through B vitamins, potassium, and magnesium, all of which have been shown to help reduce high blood pressure.

Corn and Leek Chowder

½ cup sunflower seeds
*1 cup white **corn**, removed from*
*   the cob*
white part of 1 leek
1 teaspoon raw honey
½ avocado
¼ teaspoon coriander
sea salt to taste
2 cups water
parsley for garnish

Grind sunflower seeds in a coffee grinder or dry Vita-Mix. Combine ground sunflower seeds, ½ cup corn, and remaining ingredients in a blender or Vita-Mix. Blend until very creamy and smooth. Place remaining kernels of corn in a serving bowl. Pour soup mixture into the bowl and stir. Garnish with parsley before serving.

CORN

Native Americans developed corn from seed-bearing grass over several centuries. Corn had been a major crop for them at least 2000 years before Europeans came to the New World. It featured in the change of some tribes from nomadic to agrarian especially in the Northeast. The Pawtuxet tribe, part of the larger Narragansett Indian tribe in Massachusetts, taught the Pilgrim fathers how to grow corn, pound it into meal, and cook it. It was served at the first Thanksgiving.

Corn, although a grain, must be eaten freshly picked because, once it has been removed from the stalk, the sugar content rapidly turns to starch. Corn is rich in many vitamins, but does not have a high mineral content. Corn is high in potassium and contains vitamin A, vitamin C, protein and iron, as well as fiber. It should be eaten in season but is not a valuable staple for the diet.

Studies at Illinois State University have shown that eating a low-fat diet plus 20 grams (less than a teaspoon) of corn bran each day for six weeks decreased the blood fats that contribute to heart disease by 13 percent. Those who ate wheat bran showed no such change. The soluble fiber in corn binds with cholesterol in bile from the liver. It then passes from the body, taking the cholesterol with it.

Spinach-Tomato Soup

2 cups tomato juice, freshly squeezed
½ bell pepper, chopped
1 clove garlic
2 rounded tablespoons raw tahini
1 tablespoon kelp powder
sea salt to taste
1 cup **spinach,** *chopped*
2 green onions, finely chopped

Add tomato juice, bell pepper, garlic, tahini, kelp powder, and sea salt in a blender. Blend well. Place chopped spinach and green onion in a serving bowl. Pour the blended mixture over the spinach and green onion. Stir and serve.

SPINACH

Spinach originally came from northern Asia and is now one of the most cultivated green vegetables. Spinach comes in three leaf types: smooth, semisavoy (somewhat crinkled), and savoy (crinkled). Spinach can be juiced with other vegetables for a healthy drink. It is also good chopped and added to many different dishes, or blended into raw soups.

Raw spinach is an excellent food for detoxifying the digestive tract and restoring pH balance. It is rich in minerals, especially iron. A study from the Harvard School of Public Health has found that eating at least two servings per week of spinach and other dark leafy greens may significantly cut the risk of developing cataracts. The high lutein content of spinach also helps prevent macular degeneration.

Researchers have identified at least 13 different flavonoid compounds in spinach that function as antioxidants and as anti-cancer agents. The vitamin K in spinach leaves helps maintain bone health. Vitamin K_1 activates osteocalcin, the major non-collagen protein in bone. Osteocalcin anchors calcium molecules inside of the bone. Without enough vitamin K_1, osteocalcin levels are inadequate, and bone mineralization is impaired.

All in all, spinach is an excellent disease-fighting food. Eating spinach is helps lower one's risk of heart disease, stroke, age-related macular degeneration, cataracts, and many types of cancer.

Broccoli Cream Soup

Cream
2 cups pine nuts
1 cup distilled water

To prepare cream: Soak pine nuts overnight. Rinse and drain. Place the nuts in a blender or Vita-Mix. Add 1 cup of water and blend to a fine cream. Let sit at room temperature for 12 hours. You will see the cream rising to the top, leaving the whey on the bottom. Refrigerate for several hours to allow cream to solidify.

Broccoli Soup
1 cup broccoli florets
½ cup raw cashews, soaked overnight
½ small onion, chopped
½ avocado
2 strips kelp
1 tablespoon raw honey
¼ cup fresh parsley
sea salt to taste
2 cups water or as needed

To prepare soup: Mix all ingredients in a blender until a smooth mixture is produced. To serve, scoop cream carefully off the top and use it for garnish on the broccoli soup. Serve immediately, as soup will become bitter if kept longer.

KELP

Kelp, one of several varieties of sea vegetable, is light brown to dark green in color. Kelp is the most common seaweed. It is a rich source of vitamins, especially B vitamins. It is considered valuable to brain tissue, the membranes surrounding the brain, sensory nerves, the spinal cord, and blood vessels.

It is used in thyroid treatment because of its iodine content. Kelp may be helpful in treating hair loss, obesity, and ulcers. It has 30 minerals thought to be essential to glandular health and functional as enzyme co-factors. It also helps in digestion.

Kelp is rich in minerals, and powdered kelp can be used in place of salt.

One of seaweed's most prominent health benefits is its ability to remove radioactive strontium and other heavy metals from our bodies. Whole brown seaweeds (not granulated) such as kelp contain alginic acid, which binds with the toxins in the intestines, rendering them indigestible and clearing out the intestines.

Eating seaweed promotes healthy hair growth. I always try to incorporate kelp into my diet.

Russian Borscht

½ cup walnuts, soaked overnight
juice of 1 medium beet and 5 carrots
¼ teaspoon ginger powder
1 tablespoon raw honey
sea salt to taste
½ medium onion, minced
*2 tablespoons white **sauerkraut***
½ cup shredded beets
½ cup shredded carrots

Combine walnuts, beet/carrot juice, ginger, honey, and sea salt in a blender or Vita-Mix and liquefy. Pour into a large bowl. Add onion, sauerkraut, shredded beets, and carrots. Stir ingredients until vegetables are well coated. Serve.

SAUERKRAUT

The benefits of sauerkraut have been known for generations, and it is a staple food in many European countries as well as my native Russia. Sauerkraut is fat-free. It also is low in calories. It provides almost one-third of the USRDA for vitamin C, plus other important nutrients including iron, calcium, potassium, phosphorus, thiamin, riboflavin, and niacin. One cup also provides approximately 8 grams of fiber. It is rich in cruciferous phytochemicals, which have long been proven to have disease fighting powers.

A high concentration of lactic acid in sauerkraut supports the digestive process, and assists in the maintenance of intestinal flora. The presence of acetylcholine in sauerkraut contributes to its natural laxative effect. Eating sauerkraut has a cleansing effect on the whole digestive system and promotes a feeling of well being. It also helps support the liver.

Sauerkraut is packed with cancer-fighting compounds. Fermented cabbage could be an even healthier food than raw cabbage. The results of a study published in the *Journal of Agricultural and Food Chemistry* of October 2002 concluded that sauerkraut is a cancer inhibitor. The study discovered that the fermentation of cabbage in sauerkraut produces a substance called isothiocyanates, which prevents cancer growth, particularly in the breast, colon, lung, and liver.

I give the recipe for sauerkraut in my first book, **Your Right to Be Beautiful.**

Regina's Borscht

1 cucumber, diced
1 medium beet root, shredded
*tops of **Swiss chard greens,** cut into*
  strips
1 avocado
water from 1 coconut
1 clove of garlic
2 tablespoons lemon juice
1 tablespoon soaked pistachios
sea salt to taste
1 tablespoon chopped dill

Cut half of the avocado into cubes. Combine cucumber, beet root, chard, and cubed avocado into a medium bowl and set aside. Place the other half of the avocado, coconut water, garlic, lemon juice, pistachios, and sea salt into a blender or Vita-Mix and blend until smooth. Pour the contents of the blender into the bowl. Garnish with dill and serve.

SWISS CHARD GREENS

Chard can be traced back to the hanging gardens of ancient Babylon. Native to the Mediterranean, chard was known to the Greeks, who served the roots with mustard, lentils, and beans. It is mentioned by both Aristotle and Theophrastus. The Romans introduced it to central and northern Europe

Swiss chard is grown for its large, fleshy leaves, which are coarser than spinach. Chard comes in red, green, and rainbow. It belongs to the beet family and has a similar delicate taste.

The stalks and leaves are both edible. The stalks can be used like celery or asparagus. The leaves can be used raw in salads.

Swiss chard is fat-free and cholesterol-free. It is low in sodium and calories but high in vitamins A and C, and it is loaded with calcium, iron, and fiber. All varieties of greens are naturally low in carbohydrates.

Swiss chard is sold in health food stores and some grocery stores.

I usually use the stalks for juicing and the leaves for salads, spreads, and soups.

Asparagus-Cucumber Soup

1 cup asparagus, coarsely chopped
½ cup pistachios, soaked for several hours
1 tablespoon lemon juice
sea salt to taste
dulse flakes to taste
water from 1 coconut
1 cup fresh cucumber, cubed
1 green onion, chopped
3 tablespoons minced fresh **parsley**

This recipe requires only the tender tops of asparagus, so cut off about 2-3 inches from the end. You can use the ends for juicing.

In a blender, combine tops of asparagus, pistachios, lemon juice, sea salt, dulse flakes, and water from one coconut. Blend until smooth. Add cucumber cubes and green onion and blend again lightly. Garnish soup with parsley.

PARSLEY

Parsley probably originated in Southern Europe. It was thought to possess magical properties, hence the incantation "parsley, sage, rosemary, and thyme." The ancient Greeks wore garlands of parsley to stimulate the brain and the appetite. Parsley was a sacred burial herb among the Romans. They placed it on graves and served it at funeral banquets. That practice may have been the origin of its use as a garnish — cheering thought!

Parsley has now achieved standing as a natural healing food. Research shows that parsley increases the flow of urine. Frequently referred to as diuretic, parsley is technically an "aquaretic" because it removes only water from the body, not sodium, which is a much safer way to remove excess water.

The flavonoids in parsley — especially luteolin — work as antioxidants that combine with highly reactive oxygen-containing molecules to help prevent oxygen-based damage to cells. Parsley is an excellent source of vitamin C, beta-carotene, and folic acid, all of which aid the immune system and promote cardiovascular health.

I always keep a bunch of parsley in the refrigerator and use it abundantly in my recipes.

Appetizers

Nut or Seed Cheese

2 cups nuts or seeds
(pine nuts, cashews, macadamia nuts,
    sunflower seeds, or others)
2 tablespoons lemon juice
2-3 cups water (enough to liberally cover
    nuts or seeds)
sea salt *to taste*

Soak nuts or seeds overnight. Soaking and sprouting nuts or seeds for 1–2 days before fermenting ensures that the phytic acid and enzyme inhibitors are more thoroughly removed. The alternative to soaking is to grind them dry. This will produce a more nutty flavor.

Rinse nuts or seeds well. Place in blender with water. Add the rest of the ingredients. Blend to a fine cream. Pour cream into a cheese bag. Hang the bag over the sink and allow to drain and ferment at room temperature for 6 to 8 hours or overnight. If you leave it out longer, the cheese will develop a stronger flavor. Transfer cheese to a glass storage jar and refrigerate.

Alternative method: Pour cream into a sieve. Place the sieve on the top of a container to allow water to drain off. Cover with a towel and leave for 6 to 8 hours or overnight on the counter for fermentation to take place. When the nut cheese is ready, it should smell cheesy. This cheese will keep in the refrigerator for up to a week.

SEA SALT

Regular table salt must be eliminated from your diet completely. Sea salt is a much better choice. In the raw food movement two types of sea salt are recommended: Celtic sea salt and Himalayan salt.

Celtic sea salt can be purchased from most health food stores. For more information on Himalayan salt visit *www.himalayansalt.com* or call 1-866-SALT LAMP.

However, I no longer use *any* salt in my diet. The body needs organic sodium, not inorganic salt. In my first book *Your Right to Be Beautiful* in the chapter, "The Salt of Beauty Is No Salt," I explain in great details the importance of maintaining the proper potassium/sodium balance in the body and how restriction of salt intake will result in dramatic improvement of your appearance. I believe that all the sodium that the body needs comes from fruits, vegetables or seaweed.

For the recipes in this book, I include sea salt as an ingredient, but as you become more proficient in preparing raw food dishes from "scratch," I encourage you to make your own seasoning. I use the following mix to add a salty taste to my dishes:

Homemade Celery Seasoning

> *1 bunch of celery, cut in small chunks*
> *1 lemon, peeled and sliced*
> *1 large ripe tomato, sliced*

Dehydrate celery, lemon, and tomato. Place the dehydrated ingredients in a coffee grinder or dry Vita-Mix and grind until a uniform, coarse powder is produced.

The mix is absolutely delicious! You will be tempted to eat it by itself. It tastes salty, with a slight celery flavor.

I keep this in a jar on the kitchen counter and add as needed to raw soups, crackers, guacamole, pâtés, etc.

Gratinée of Cauliflower

½ medium cauliflower head, cored and
   cut into small chunks
2 gloves garlic, finely chopped
1 cup **pine nut** cheese
2 tablespoons lemon juice
sea salt to taste
2 cups coconut water
2 tablespoon fresh parsley, chopped

Place the pine nut cheese, cauliflower, garlic, sea salt, and coconut water in a food processor fitted with a steel blade and process until the mixture is coarsely pureed. Remove the mixture from the food processor, place in a bowl, and add parsley. Tastes delicious served on crackers, carrots, or celery sticks.

PINE NUTS

The pine nut was once a staple food for the people of Africa and Australia. In Europe, the Middle East, and Asia, pine nuts have been eaten since the earliest recorded times, probably before the introduction of agriculture. Many Native Americans gathered pine nuts annually and stored them to be eaten throughout the long winter months.

Pine nuts are probably the most neglected fine eating nuts in the U.S., even though they are both plentiful and high in nutrition. Pine nuts, produced by many varieties of pine trees, are near the top of the list of wholesome foods and can be found all over the world.

Nuts generally contain high quantities of good fats that help lower cholesterol. They are also an excellent source of vitamin A, vitamin B_6, dietary fiber, thiamin, niacin, and iron. All of these are essential for maintaining a healthy system and help in lowering cholesterol and blood pressure, and reducing the risk of heart disease.

Gamma-linolenic acid (GLA) is the active component in pine nuts. GLA has been clinically proven to be an effective natural remedy against many diseases. Hundreds of clinical studies have indicated that GLA can cure or alleviate diverse health problems ranging from rheumatoid arthritis and high blood pressure to premenstrual syndrome (PMS). All of these conditions, in most people, are caused by essential fatty acid deficiencies.

Beet Root Delight

3 medium beet roots, peeled and
  finely shredded
3 tablespoons lemon juice
*½ cup **macadamia** cheese*
1 avocado
3 Medjool dates, pits removed
½ cup walnuts, crushed
2 cloves of garlic, minced
sea salt to taste

Combine shredded beet roots and lemon juice in a bowl and set aside. Place macadamia cheese, avocado, and dates into a food processor and puree until creamy. Transfer the mixture to a bowl. Add the remaining ingredients and mix well with a spoon until the mixture is of uniform consistency. Serve on crackers or on a bed of romaine lettuce.

MACADAMIA NUTS

Macadamia nuts are on the growing list of healthy nuts like walnuts, almonds, and pecans. A study from the University of Hawaii shows that a diet containing high-fat nuts can actually improve cholesterol levels.

Blood fat analysis showed that the cholesterol levels of those who included macadamia nuts in their diets were similar to those of people who followed the standard low-fat diet. The potent antioxidants inn macadamia nuts help to protect against cancer and heart disease.

The nuts contain no cholesterol and are low in sodium and saturated fats. An ounce of macadamias (about eleven nuts) may have as much as two grams of protein. They also contain vitamin A, thiamine, riboflavin, niacin, and iron.

The macadamia nut is one of the few foods that contains palmitoleic acid, a monounsaturated fatty acid. In a recent study, indicators suggest that palmitoleic acid may actually aid fat metabolism, possibly reducing stored body fat.

I exercise with weights at least twice per week and I believe that eating macadamia nuts is essential to people following the raw food diet to ensure that they build good quality muscles.

Cucumber Stuffed with Corn & Cashew Cheese

4 narrow pickled cucumbers
1 cup corn kernels
*1 cup **cashew** cheese*
2 tablespoons chives, minced
1 tablespoon fresh dill, minced

Halve cucumbers and scoop out seeds, forming cavities. Coarsely puree corn and cashew cheese in a food processor. Add chives. Fill cucumber halves with mixture, mounding slightly, and sprinkle with dill. Serve immediately.

CASHEWS

In addition to their healthful monounsaturated fats, cashews are a good source of copper, zinc, and magnesium. Copper is an essential component of many enzymes that play a role in iron utilization, free-radical elimination, developing bone and connective tissue, and producing melanin in the skin and hair.

Cashews are a good source of zinc, which benefits the immune system. Zinc is also critical to normal cell division. Zinc helps stabilize blood sugar levels and the body's metabolic rate, enhancing senses of smell and taste.

Cashews contain magnesium, which, like calcium, is necessary for healthy bones. About two-thirds of the magnesium in the human body is in the bones. Magnesium helps to balance calcium, regulating nerve and muscle tone. By blocking calcium, magnesium keeps our nerves relaxed.

Most cashews are roasted. The cashews labeled "raw" are not really raw, they are simply "not roasted." They have been steamed out of their shells. There is a toxic resin inside the shell; therefore, unless the shell is opened properly, this toxic resin will contaminate the nut, making it inedible. The most common means of opening the shell is to steam it at a high temperature — so it is, essentially, cooked.

Nature's First Law uses a special technique without heat to open the shell cleanly without exposing the cashew to the resin. The raw cashews are much sweeter, tastier, and nutritious than their cooked counterparts. A truly raw cashew will sprout.

*I buy my cashews from **www.rawfood.com**, which is a source for Nature's First Law products.*

Primavera Pistachio Pâté on Romaine Lettuce

1 cup **pistachios,** *soaked overnight
and skinned*
½ *cup sun-dried tomatoes, soaked for
several hours*
1 *stalk of celery, minced*
1 *bell pepper, finely chopped*
sea salt to taste
2 *green onions, minced*
½ *cup fresh parsley, minced*
4 *hearts Romaine Lettuce*

Combine pistachios, sun-dried tomatoes, celery, bell pepper, and sea salt in a food processor fitted with an "S" blade. Pulse until a coarse mixture is formed. Transfer mixture to a bowl. Stir in green onions and fresh parsley. Peel leaves from each head of romaine lettuce and fill them with the mixture from the food processor. Serve.

PISTACHIOS

Pistachios grew wild in the high desert regions of the Holy Lands. They were supposedly such a favorite of the Queen of Sheba that she kept the entire crop for herself and her court. According to one legend, lovers met under the trees because the sound of the nuts cracking meant good fortune. Pistachios appeared in the United States in the 1880s, primarily for the Middle Eastern market, but they soon became popular with everyone.

Pistachios, like other tree nuts, have many health benefits. Although pistachios contain high levels of fats, most of the fat content is monounsaturated, significantly reducing the risk for heart disease.

Among all tree nuts, pistachios contain the highest level of phytosterols, which are directly associated with lowering cholesterol levels and may offer protection from certain types of cancer. Also, like other nuts, pistachios are high in both calcium and magnesium.

Research has found that eating two ounces of pistachios a day helps adults lower their cholesterol levels. Substituting pistachios or other nuts for snacks can lower cholesterol levels by almost 10 percent.

Pistachios are my favorite nuts. I like to eat them soaked for breakfast with my morning juice.

Stuffed Cherry Tomatoes with Macadamia Cheese

20 to 25 cherry tomatoes
1 cup macadamia cheese
2 tablespoons green onions, minced
2 tablespoons celery, minced
cayenne pepper to taste
sea salt to taste
20 to 25 black **olive** *slices for garnish*
2 tablespoons parsley, minced, for garnish
a few washed lettuce leaves for garnish

Wash the cherry tomatoes. Open the top of each tomato, being careful not to remove the top completely; leave it attached as a lid. Remove the pulp, drain well, and put shells aside for stuffing. Save tomato pulp to use for something else.

Combine macadamia cheese, green onions, celery, cayenne pepper, and sea salt in a bowl. Mix well. Fill the cherry tomatoes with the stuffing. Decorate each with a black olive slice and parsley. Half close with the attached tomato lid and arrange stuffed tomatoes on a bed of lettuce. Makes 20 to 25 stuffed tomatoes.

Chef's Tip: *Macadamia Cheese mixture may be spooned into a pastry bag. Choose a decorative tip and pipe mixture into the cherry tomatoes.*

OLIVES

After the Flood, Noah sent a dove out of the ark, to see if the land was dry enough to disembark. The second time the dove was sent out, she returned with an olive leaf in her mouth, indicating that the water was abated and God's great judgment was past. Ever since, the dove and the olive branch have been a sign of peace.

Olives are fruits with a single large seed. They are picked at various stages of ripeness from a variety of trees to yield different colors, tastes, and textures. Unripe olives are green, with very bitter, firm flesh. As they ripen, they become oilier and darker. Fully ripe olives are either deep green, brown, or black from being oxidized by the sun. Other olives are picked unripe, then oxidize during processing.

Olives and their oil are rich in monounsaturated fat. This type of fat lowers artery-clogging cholesterol while maintaining — or raising — favorable cholesterol levels. Research suggests that the monounsaturated fat in olives may also help protect against diabetes and certain cancers. Olives also are a very good source of vitamin E and calcium.

Raw olives are more bitter than processed ones. All commercial olives undergo a curing process to remove bitter compounds. The best place to buy certified organic raw olives is *www.rawdiet.com*. They are uncured and contain no salt, oil, or herbs.

Olives are packed with health-inducing minerals. In nature, high nutrition content and bitter flavors go hand in hand. Olives may be enjoyed straight from the jar; however, if you want to mellow the bitterness, soak the olives in water for several hours. This reduces the bitterness by 50 percent.

Garbanzo Bean Hummus

*1 cup **garbanzo beans (chickpeas)***
½ cup pine nuts, soaked for several hours
3 tablespoons freshly squeezed lemon juice
2 cloves garlic
½ cup fresh parsley, chopped
sea salt to taste
1 cup coconut water

Soak garbanzo beans for one day, changing water twice during the day. Sprout beans for two days.

Combine all ingredients in Vita-Mix and blend until smooth. More coconut water may be added if mixture is too thick. Refrigerate before serving.

Best served with raw carrot or celery sticks.

GARBANZO BEANS

"Chickpea" and "garbanzo bean" are two names for the same thing. *Garbanzo* is the name used in Spanish speaking countries. The English name *chickpea* comes from the French *chiche,* which comes from the Latin *cicer.*

Garbanzo beans are rich in soluble fiber — the most beneficial type of fiber — which helps to eliminate cholesterol from the body. They are rich in carbohydrates, proteins, phosphorus, calcium, and iron. They are also a useful source of folate, vitamin E, potassium, manganese, copper, and zinc. As a high-potassium, low-sodium food they help reduce blood pressure.

Garbanzo beans or chickpeas are the most widely consumed legume in the world. They have a firm texture with a flavor somewhere between chestnuts and walnuts.

Beans are high in fiber and protein, yet low in fat. They also contain vitamins, minerals, and other important nutrients. Research suggests that beans can help fight heart disease, diabetes, high cholesterol, and some types of cancer. Beans also make you feel full without adding a lot of extra calories to the meal, and may, therefore, be useful in losing weight or fighting weight gain.

Kale Guacamole

*3 leaves of lacinato **kale***
2 small avocados
3 dates, pitted
2 strips of kelp soaked for 10 minutes
2 tablespoons lemon juice
sea salt to taste
2 cloves garlic, chopped
1 small tomato, small diced
½ cup fresh parsley, finely chopped

Place kale, avocados, dates, kelp, garlic, lemon juice, and sea salt into the food processor fitted with a steel blade and mix until creamy. Stir in tomato and parsley. Serve on crackers.

KALE

Kale and collards go back for at least two thousand years. The Greeks grew both, although they made no distinction between them. The Romans cultivated several varieties well before the time of Christ. The Romans may have introduced the *coles,* as they were called, to Britain and France, although their wide availability makes it possible that they may have arrived with the Celts. They probably came to Colonial America very early.

Like most members of the *Brassica* family, kale is descended from sea cabbage, which gives it the characteristic waxy, moisture-retaining leaves. It can be grown from Florida to Alaska with very little effort — it seems to thrive on neglect.

Kale has over ten times the vitamin A as the same amount of iceberg lettuce. Served in equivalent portions it has more vitamin C than orange juice and more calcium than cow's milk.

Kale's concentrated beta-carotene content is an excellent source of vitamin A, which helps prevent premature aging. One cup of kale provides almost 250 percent of the daily value for vitamin A. Both vitamin A and beta-carotene are important vision nutrients. Kale contains the antioxidant lutein and iron, which transports oxygen to the skin.

Kale has manganese and calcium, among other healthy attributes. Calcium is one of the nutrients needed to make healthy bones. But kale, unlike dairy products, is not a highly allergenic food, nor does it contain any saturated fat.

I use lacinato kale (also known as black cabbage, dinosaur kale, or Italian heirloom) in my recipes because of its smoother texture.

Eggplant Caviar

2 cups water
2 tablespoons sea salt
*2 cups **eggplant**, peeled and cubed*
1 cup sun-dried tomatoes, soaked for
   several hours
2 strips kelp
1 tablespoon lemon juice
¼ cup olive oil
1 small onion, minced
¼ cup roughly chopped fresh
   flat-leaf parsley

Combine 2 cups water and 2 tablespoons of sea salt in a large bowl. Place eggplant cubes in the liquid. Place a plate on top of the cubes to keep them from floating. Marinate overnight.

Strain eggplant very well and squeeze out (by hand or by using a press) as much water as possible. Combine all ingredients, except parsley and onion, in a food processor fitted with a steel blade and process until it is coarsely pureed. Stir parsley and onion into mixture. Serve on crackers, or on the leaves of romaine lettuce or Belgian endive.

EGGPLANT

Records from as early as 500 B.C. indicate that eggplant was cultivated in China, although it is uncertain where it originated. The Moors introduced it to Spain, but it was slow to gain popularity in Europe, where it was known as "mad apple." It does belong to the deadly nightshade family and can cause illness unless it is fully mature. There are, however, no known cases of fatality.

Eggplant has minimal vitamin content (though it does contain vitamin A, folacin, and vitamin C), but it is low in calories and sodium and provides calcium, magnesium, potassium, and phosphorus in large enough quantities to recommend keeping it in your diet. Eggplant also contains the phytochemical *monoterpene,* which may be helpful in preventing the growth of cancer cells.

Research on eggplant has focused on an anthocyanin phytonutrient found in eggplant skin called *nasunin. Nasunin* is a potent antioxidant and free radical scavenger that has been shown to protect cell membranes from damage.

To boost the nutritional benefits, pair eggplant with other vegetables such as tomatoes, onions, and peppers.

Portobello Pâté

*3 medium **portobello mushrooms,** diced*
1 cup Nama Shoyu
1 cup water
½ red bell pepper
½ medium sweet onion
1 stalk celery

In a large bowl, toss mushrooms with Nama Shoyu and water. Cover bowl with a plate to keep mushrooms from floating. Allow to marinate for 1 to 3 hours on kitchen counter. Discard the marinade or reserve for more mushrooms or onion slices.

Combine all ingredients in a food processor fitted with an "S" blade. Process until coarse, yet smooth. Excellent served on Essene bread or with vegetable sticks.

PORTOBELLO MUSHROOMS

According to 4,600-year-old hieroglyphics, ancient Egyptians believed that portobello mushrooms were the plant of immortality. As usual with royalty from Egypt to Europe, if anything was good to eat, it became the sole property of the royal house and was denied to commoners.

Many countries practiced mushroom rituals, especially in instances where hallucinations from mushrooms were connected to religious rites. Many believed that mushrooms had properties that could produce super-human strength, help in finding lost objects, and lead the soul on a vision quest.

Although mushrooms are often grouped with vegetables and fruits, they are actually fungi — for that reason, they are in a class of their own, nutritionally speaking. Mushrooms do share some of the benefits of fruits and vegetables. They are low in calories, have no cholesterol, and are virtually free of fat and sodium.

Mushrooms contain some essential minerals and B-complex vitamins that do not appear regularly in fruits and vegetables. They contain a high quantity of potassium, which helps maintain normal heart rhythm, muscle and nerve function. Copper, an essential mineral that regulates iron's role in delivering oxygen to the cells, is found in mushrooms.

Current tests suggest that mushrooms help lower cancer risks, high blood cholesterol, and high blood pressure.

Alternate spelling, *portobella.*

Note: Portobello mushrooms are the mature form of the crimino mushroom, which is a variation of the commonly cultivated white mushroom. The name "portobello" was invented in the 1980s as part of a marketing ploy to popularize this difficult-to-sell mushroom.

Asparagus Nori Wrap

*10 asparagus spears, bottom
    ends trimmed*
1 cup Nama Shoyu
1 cup macadamia cheese
2 tablespoon lemon juice
1 tablespoon olive oil
*10 **nori** sheets*
2 medium red bell pepper, cut in strips

Marinate trimmed asparagus spears in Nama Shoyu for several hours. Combine macadamia cheese with lemon juice and olive oil in a small bowl. Divide and spread the mixture evenly on half of each nori sheet. Place one piece of asparagus and several strips of red pepper on the edge of each nori sheet. Roll the nori sheet, and secure by sealing with a little water on your finger. Cut into bite-sized pieces to serve.

NORI

Nori is one of several varieties of sea vegetable. It is a dark, purple-black color that turns fluorescent green when toasted. Nori is mainly cultivated on nets in the sea on which the seaweed takes root and grows. Nori is harvested by picking it from the nets and washing it thoroughly. It is then chopped finely and spread onto flat meshes to dry.

Nori is best known as "the flat, black thing that wraps up sushi." It looks like nothing more than black paper, but one sheet has many healthy attributes. It contains a variety of vitamins. The vitamin A in two sheets of nori is the equivalent of 45 grams of spinach. Vitamin A is good for the skin, teeth and hair. It also contains substantial amounts of vitamins B_1 and B_2. The amount of vitamin C in nori is twice as much as in the same amount of lemon.

Nori, like all other seaweed, is a rich source of calcium, zinc, and iodine. Nori is an excellent source of iron, which helps prevent anemia. It is also a good source of lignins which help fight cancer.

This power food is an invaluable addition to the raw food diet.

Entrées

Rainbow "Macaroni" with Red Marinara

Red Marinara Sauce
½ cup **flax seed,** soaked overnight
2 strips dry kelp, soaked for
    15 to 30 minutes
2 cups sun-dried tomatoes, soaked for
    several hours
2 avocados, pitted
2 Medjool dates, pitted
2 cloves garlic with skin on
sea salt to taste
2 large tomatoes, diced

To make red marinara: Mix flax seed, kelp, sun-dried tomatoes, avocados, dates, garlic, and sea salt in the Vita-Mix until creamy. Pour the mixture into a container. Add diced tomato.

To make rainbow macaroni: Spiralize zucchini, beet root, carrots, and turnip. Make into live "noodles" by using a spiral slicer (saladacco).

Serve red marinara over rainbow macaroni.

Flax Seed

The ancient Greeks and Romans valued flax seed for its laxative effects and its ability to relieve gastric distress. Today, consumers still use flax seed for its laxative and other health benefits: lowering blood cholesterol and protecting against heart disease, stroke, and, possibly, certain types of cancer.

It is probably the richest source of the essential Omega-3 fatty acids in the North American diet. Flax seed is particularly rich in lignins, a special compound also found in other seeds, grains, and legumes. These hormone-like agents have shown a number of protective effects against breast cancer. For this reason, flax seed and flax seed flour are being studied for their contributions to women's health.

Flax seed has been shown to lower serum cholesterol levels. It lowers blood lipid levels because of its soluble fiber content and its very low saturated fat content.

Gabriel Cousens, M.D., believes that the addition of flax seed to the diet is very important for vegetarians and especially for people following the raw food lifestyle. According to his book *Conscious Eating,* the Omega-3s in flax seeds will "contribute to smoother skin, shinier hair, softer hands, smoother muscle action, the normalization of blood sugar, increased cold weather resistance, and generally improved immune system."

I often simply grind whole, dry flax seed in a coffee grinder or Vita-Mix and eat it directly or sprinkle it on my salad.

Meatless "Meatballs" Nested in Live Macaroni

½ cup flax seed
2 strips of kelp, soaked for 10 minutes
1 cup sun-dried tomatoes, soaked
   for an hour
½ cup walnuts
½ bell pepper, cut into small pieces
1 stalk of celery, chopped
1 tablespoon whole psyllium husk
1 cup ground **pumpkin seeds**
½ cup fresh parsley
½ cup sweet onion, minced
sea salt to taste

Grind flax seed in a coffee grinder or dry Vita-Mix. Add kelp and sun-dried tomatoes to ground flax and blend well. Pour the mixture into a food processor, and add walnuts, bell pepper, and celery. Puree ingredients. Transfer to a bowl. Stir in whole psyllium husk, ground pumpkin seeds, parsley, and onion. Mix well by hand. Form into balls, using a small cookie dough scoop. Place "meatballs" on mesh dehydrator sheets, and dehydrate for 6 to 8 hours. Serve each "meatball" on a nest made from zucchini noodles.

PUMPKIN SEEDS

The seeds from your Halloween pumpkin are some of the most nutritious and flavorful seeds around. They have a sweet, nutty taste and a chewy texture. Pumpkin seeds are freshest in the fall during pumpkin season.

Pumpkin and pumpkin seeds are being used as a deterrent to prostate problems in men. The seeds contain chemical substances that can prevent the body from converting testosterone into a much more potent form, which causes problems with the prostate.

The properties of pumpkin seeds as an anti-inflammatory for arthritis have been recently investigated. Unlike some drugs, pumpkin seeds do not increase the level of damaged fats (lipid peroxides) in the linings of the joints, a side-effect that actually contributes to the progression of arthritis.

Healthy Buckwheat "Burger"

"Burger" Buns
1 cup buckwheat, soaked and sprouted
*1 cup **sunflower seeds,** soaked overnight*
½ cup sun-dried tomatoes, soaked for
   several hours
½ medium red onion, minced
2 tablespoons whole psyllium husk
¼ cup fresh parsley, finely chopped
a pinch of paprika
sea salt to taste

Combine buckwheat, sunflower seeds, and sun-dried tomatoes in a food processor and mix well. Transfer the dough to a medium bowl. Stir in red onion, whole psyllium husk, parsley, paprika, and sea salt. Form the dough by hand into six half-inch thick buns and place on mesh dehydrator sheets. Dehydrate 12 hours, turning at least once.

"Burger"
3 medium portobello mushroom caps
1 cup Nama Shoyu
2 tablespoons lemon juice
1 large tomato, sliced
½ large onion, sliced in rings

Marinate mushrooms in Nama Shoyu and lemon juice for at least 15 minutes or up to several hours. Discard marinade.

To assemble the burger: Place one large tomato slice, onion rings to taste, and marinated mushroom between two of the buns and enjoy. Makes 3 burgers.

SUNFLOWER SEEDS

The sunflower came from South America, where it was used extensively by Native Americans for not only food and oil but also for natural dyes. It was introduced into Spain by the explorers and became one of the premiere sources of cooking oil for the world.

The sunflower is a beautiful addition to your garden and a feast for birds, and the seeds are a nutritious snack which adds flavor to salads and other dishes. The petals, however, are not edible.

The seeds are high in vitamin E, magnesium, and selenium. Their vitamin E content offers easy access to one of the best fat-soluble antioxidants which prevents cholesterol particles from building up in blood vessels and contributing to heart-related health problems.

Magnesium is also important for heart health. It is also necessary for good bones, since two-thirds of the body's magnesium is stored in the bones, where it helps maintain structure and can be drawn upon as needed. Magnesium can offset calcium, regulating nerves and muscles and keeping them relaxed. A quarter cup has almost 40 percent of the daily requirement.

That same quarter cup also contains about 40 percent of a person's daily selenium needs. Selenium is a trace mineral that helps in cancer prevention and retarding aging processes in the body.

Sunflower seeds have a low occurrence of allergic reactions.

Vibrant Veggie Nori Rolls

2 cups almonds, soaked overnight
1 medium bell pepper, cut in chunks
sea salt to taste
½ cup sunflower seeds, soaked overnight,
*   rinsed and dried*
1 stalk celery, finely minced
10 raw nori sheets (sun-dried)
2 large carrots, spiralized or cut
*   in long strips*
1 large beet, spiralized or shredded
2 avocado cut in long strips
10 green onions, sliced in half lengthwise
1 cup **alfalfa sprouts**

Combine almonds, bell pepper chunks, and sea salt in a food processor. Process until a smooth paste is formed. Remove the mixture from the food processor and place in a bowl. Stir in sunflower seeds, and minced celery. Mix well with a spoon.

Spread mixture about 1 inch wide and ¼-inch high along the short side of a nori sheet. Spread spiralized carrots, beets, avocado strips, green onion, and alfalfa sprouts along the same side. Starting with the edge closest to you, using both hands, gently roll each nori into a log. Moisten the outer edge of the nori with water to help seal it. Repeat procedure for all nori rolls. Cut the rolls into cylinders 1-inch long. Serve.

Will keep refrigerated 1–2 days.

ALFALFA

Alfalfa is one of the oldest crops grown for forage. It is thought to have originated in east of the Mediterranean in southwestern Asia. It spread to Greece and along the Silk Road to China. The Romans planted it in Spain and the Conquistadors introduced it to the New World.

Legume sprouts are very alkaline, and alfalfa sprouts are no exception. In the human body, they increase bone formation and density. They are also helpful in controlling hot flashes, menopause, PMS, and fibrocystic breast tumors.

Alfalfa sprouts contain saponins that lower "bad" cholesterol and fat but not "good" HDL fats. Saponins stimulate the immune system by increasing the activity of natural killer cells such as T-lymphocytes, and increasing the production of interferon.

Alfalfa sprouts have amino acids that boost immunity to pancreatic, colon, and leukemia cancers. They have strong antioxidants and are a good source of vitamin C, folate, vitamin A, niacin, potassium, phosphorus, calcium, magnesium.

Pasta Primavera with Pesto

Pesto

1 cup raw pine nuts, soaked for several
*   hours*
*¼ cup **basil leaves**, finely chopped*
½ cup olive oil
2 cloves garlic
2 teaspoons lemon juice
1 teaspoon raw honey
sea salt to taste

Mix all ingredients in a food processor. Toss with Live Macaroni made from zucchini, spiralized with a spiral slicer (saladacco). Serve.

BASIL LEAVES

A smell of Basil is good for the heart and head — cureth the infirmities of the heart, taketh away sorrowfulness which cometh of melancholia and maketh a man merry and glad.
— John Gerard

Basil originated in India and Persia. Its name means "be fragrant." Despite this name, ancient cultures gave it mixed reviews. It was scorned by the Greeks, who considered it a symbol of hate, but it was prized by the Romans, who used it as a symbol of love and fertility. Traditionally, if a Roman boy accepted a sprig from a girl, they were considered engaged. Today, Hindus plant it for happiness.

Basil, a bright green, leafy plant from the mint family, has a sweet, herbal bouquet that complements vegetables. Like all green vegetables, it is rich in vitamin C. It is used for seasoning and to enhance the taste of other ingredients rather than as a major dietary source in itself.

Eggplant Pizza

2 to 3 cups water
2 teaspoons sea salt
1 medium eggplant, peeled
1 cup **watercress**
3 stalks celery, cut in chunks
1 clove garlic
2 cups macadamia cheese
1 tablespoon Italian seasoning
1 large, ripe tomato, thinly sliced
several olives, sliced

Slice eggplant into thin circles and soak in salty water overnight. Drain and rinse well. Place watercress, celery, garlic, and sea salt in a food processor and blend well. Add macadamia cheese and blend again until creamy. Spread the mixture evenly on top of each eggplant slice. Place a thin slice of tomato and a slice of olive on top of eggplant pizza. Dehydrate for 8 hours.

WATERCRESS

Watercress seems to have been one of the determining factors in choosing the site of the very first hospital. Hipprocates, considered the father of modern medicine, chose his location because it gave him access to a stream where he could get fresh watercress for treating his patients. Watercress grows in gravel beds in flowing spring water.

In early 19th century England, watercress was a staple of the working class diet, often being used in breakfast sandwiches. Those too poor to afford bread ate their watercress plain. For that reason, it became known as "poor man's bread." It was grown commercially in the chalk streams of Hampshire and Dorset. Street sellers then bought it loose at Covent Garden and gathered it into bunches. It was eaten much like an ice-cream cone. It is one of the street vendor's cries from Dickens's *Oliver Twist.*

The plant is useful for skin and blood disorders, jaundice, and kidney conditions. Like parsley, watercress is an excellent source of vitamins C, A, E, D, K, and the B vitamins. Watercress contains three times as much vitamin C as lettuce and is rich in sodium, potassium, and calcium, plus sulfur, iron, copper, and manganese, minerals which strengthen the blood.

Its high vitamin C content makes it an excellent food choice for the elderly because it sustains flexibility in the small blood vessels, helping to protect against hardening of the arteries. Watercress appears to have the potential for preventing the development of cancers of the lung and breast.

Lusty Luxurious Lasagna

Basil and Hemp "Ricotta"
*2 cups **hemp seeds** or macadamia cheese*
2 tablespoons lemon juice
2 cups packed basil leaves
sea salt to taste

Place all ingredients in a food processor and pulse a few times until thoroughly combined. Add a little water, as needed, and pulse until the mixture becomes fluffy. Place in a bowl, cover, and set aside.

Marengo Sauce
2 cups sun-dried tomatoes, soaked
*   for an hour and drained*
½ small onion, chopped
2 tablespoons lemon juice
1 tablespoon raw honey
6 tablespoons olive oil
sea salt to taste
pinch of Cayenne pepper
1 medium ripe tomato, diced

Place all ingredients except diced tomato in a blender or Vita-Mix, and blend until smooth. Place the mixture in a bowl. Add tomato. Cover and set aside.

Lasagna
3 medium zucchini, ends trimmed
3 medium ripe tomatoes
3 tablespoons fresh parsley, finely chopped
3 tablespoons fresh oregano, finely
*   chopped*
whole basil leaves to garnish

Shave zucchini lengthwise into very thin slices. Cut tomatoes in half, and then into thin slices. Line the bottom of a 9x13 inch baking dish with two layers of zucchini slices. Spread one third of the Marengo sauce over it, and top with one third of the ricotta. Cover with one third of the tomato slices. Sprinkle with oregano and parsley, using one tablespoon of each. Add another two layers of zucchini and repeat the layers of Marengo sauce, ricotta, tomato slices, and herbs. Repeat. Garnish with basil.

HEMP SEEDS

Hemp is one of the oldest crops known. George Washington and Thomas Jefferson are thought to have cultivated it. The Declaration of Independence is written on hemp paper, and Betsy Ross sewed the original Stars and Stripes using hemp fiber.

Hemp grown for food consumption contains only trace amounts of THC, the psychoactive substance in marijuana. It is a highly nutritious food. It is high in essential fatty acids, Omega-3, and GLA, and vitamin E, iron, and lecithin. Hemp contains three times as much vitamin E as flax.

Hemp seeds are an exceptionally rich source of unsaturated fatty acids. They have nearly 20 percent more essential fatty acids than flax seed. The human body does not produce Essential Fatty Acids (EFAs). It is, therefore, important that EFAs be consumed on a regular basis. EFAs are "good fats." Shelled hemp seed is comprised of 45 percent "good fats" in an ideal balance of Omega-3 alpha-linolenic acid, Omega-6 linolenic acid, Omega-3 stearidonic acid, and Omega-6 gamma linolenic acid. Hemp seeds are 33 percent protein and contain all eight amino acids. A shelled hemp seed (or hempnut) has a rich nutty flavor, similar to that of a pine nut or sunflower seed. Hemp seeds can be added to almost any recipe.

Hemp seeds are processed using a cold mechanical process. They must be refrigerated to keep them from becoming rancid. The best source for certified organic hemp seeds is *www.purefoodmarket.com.*

Mock Salmon with Red Sauce

1 cup flax seed
2 cups pumpkin seeds, soaked overnight
2 large carrots, cut in chunks
½ lemon, peeled and de-seeded
2 shallots, minced
½ medium red bell pepper, finely chopped
1 cup celery, minced
½ cup fresh parsley, minced
2 teaspoons paprika
sea salt to taste

Grind flax seed in a coffee grinder or dry Vita-Mix container. Using a Champion Juicer with the blank plate attached, process the pumpkin seeds, carrots, and lemon. Transfer the mixture to a large bowl. Stir in remaining ingredients and mix thoroughly with a spoon. Shape the mixture into a loaf. Place on a mesh dehydrating sheet and dehydrate for several hours.

Red Sauce
1 avocado
1 cup fresh tomatoes, cut into chunks
½ cup sun-dried tomatoes, soaked for
  several hours
2 Medjool dates, pitted
several basil leaves
dash of Cayenne pepper
1 clove garlic, chopped
sea salt to taste

Combine all the ingredients in a food processor and puree.

Place Mock Salmon on platter and cover with red sauce before serving.

SHALLOTS

Shallots are part of the *Allium* family, which includes onions, scallions, chives, leeks, and garlic. It is more subtle in flavor than the onion and less pungent than garlic. Unlike both of these herbs, shallots do not cause bad breath.

Researchers have found that shallots (and yellow and red onions) contain a powerful antioxidant that acts as an anticancer agent blocking the formation of cancer cells. The antioxidant quercetin deactivates the growth of estrogen-sensitive cells often found be a cause of breast cancer. White onions do not have this antioxidant.

Garlic and onions, as well as shallots, leeks, scallions, and chives contain the active compound *allicin* which is shown to significantly lower cholesterol, reduce the stickiness of blood, and widen blood vessels, helping to prevent heart disease and stroke. *Allicin* also enhances immunity, warding off bacterial and fungal infections as well as viruses.

On the raw food diet, shallots seem to be used more often than regular onions. They are milder and do not cause stomach irritation.

Live Pizza

Pizza Crust
½ cup flax seed
2 cups sunflower seeds, soaked overnight
1 teaspoon lemon juice
a pinch of cayenne pepper
sea salt to taste

Grind flax seed in coffee grinder or a dry Vita-Mix. Combine all ingredients in a food processor. Process until a uniform dough is formed. Spread the dough with a spatula onto dehydrator teflex sheets approximately ¼-inch thick. Dehydrate for 6 hours and turn over and dehydrate for an additional 6 hours. When crust is ready, cut into individual squares.

Pizza Topping
1 cup macadamia cheese
*2 tablespoons dried **oregano***
sea salt to taste
2 tablespoons fresh basil, minced
1 thick zucchini, sliced
2 cups sun-dried tomatoes, soaked for
*   several hours*

Mix macadamia cheese, oregano, and sea salt well. Spread this mixture on the individual squares of crust. Place minced basil leaf on top of each square. Slice zucchini diagonally and cut to fit the squares. Place zucchini slice on the top of each minced basil leaf. Then sprinkle with finely chopped sun-dried tomatoes and oregano. Dehydrate for additional 5 hours.

OREGANO

A member of the mint family, oregano is native to the hills of the Mediterranean regions. It is sometimes called "the pizza herb" because it became popular in the States after World War II when the GIs talked about the pizza they had eaten in Italy.

Ancient cultures considered oregano an aid to digestion. Like many beliefs this one seems to have had a basis in fact. Oregano has powerful bacteria- and fungus-killing properties, and can be used as a painkiller and anti-inflammatory.

Medicinally, oregano tea is used for indigestion and coughs, and to bring on menstruation. Oil of oregano is used for toothache.

Raw Chili

1 cup garbanzo beans
½ cup raisins (or currants)
1 cup sun-dried tomatoes
1 cup mushrooms (marinated in
  ***Nama Shoyu** for an hour)*
1 cup water
sea salt to taste
1 teaspoon cayenne pepper
1 cup celery, chopped
2 to 5 cloves garlic, minced
1 bunch basil, minced

Soak garbanzo beans overnight, then sprout for 3 days. Rinse well and set aside.

Combine raisins, sun-dried tomatoes, mushrooms, water, sea salt, and cayenne pepper in a blender or Vita-Mix and puree until smooth. Transfer the blended mixture into a large bowl and mix in the sprouted garbanzo beans, celery, garlic, and minced basil. Serve.

Nama Shoyu

Shoyu is the Japanese word for soy sauce made of soybeans, roasted wheat, sea salt, and koji (mold spores that are exposed to moisture so they begin to grow and develop unique enzymes that create the fermentation process). This is the all-purpose cooking and condiment, made since the 1600s in Japan.

True shoyu's best quality is its ability to enhance other foods. These qualities are the result of its long, slow fermentation process.

Fermentation breaks down proteins into amino acids and carbohydrates into simple sugars. This makes it easily digestible. It contains the health benefits of its sources, soybeans and wheat, but, like many garnishes and marinades, its main contribution is flavor.

Nama Shoyu is acceptable in the raw food lifestyle. Even though it was originally cooked, the fermentation process that takes place for several years creates a new living culture.

A good place to purchase Nama Shoyu is from *www.goldminenaturalfood.com.*

Snacks

Onion Rings

6 ears fresh yellow corn
1 cup sun-dried tomatoes, soaked for an
*   hour*
1 cup pistachios, soaked overnight
water, as needed
1 large sweet onion
1 teaspoon paprika to taste
***cayenne pepper** to taste*
sea salt to taste

Cut corn off each cob and place in blender or Vita-Mix. Add sun-dried tomatoes, pistachios, paprika, cayenne, sea salt, and some water if needed. Blend to the consistency of pancake batter. Thinly slice sweet onion and separate rings. Dip each onion ring into corn batter and place on a mesh dehydrating sheet. Dehydrate for 1 to 2 days.

CAYENNE PEPPER

Hot and spicy, cayenne pepper adds zest to cuisine around the world while giving better health to those who hazard its fire. The active principle that causes the heat in chili peppers is a crystalline alkaloid generically called *capsaicin*. The higher the concentration, the hotter the pepper. Cayenne is actually on the milder end of the pepper family, which is probably why it is so popular. It has long been used as a mild garnish on salads.

Capsaicin has been extensively studied for its pain-reducing effects, its cardiovascular benefits, and its ability to help prevent ulcers. Capsaicin also clears your sinuses.

Cayenne peppers are a good source of the important antioxidant beta-carotene, which is considered valuable in reducing the symptoms of asthma, osteoarthritis, and rheumatoid arthritis.

Chili peppers do not cause stomach ulcers. On the contrary, hot peppers help prevent ulcers because the capsaicin kills bacteria in the stomach while encouraging the lining to produce more of the buffering juices that prevent ulcers.

On the raw food diet, people may initially feel cold. Including cayenne pepper in your diet will help with this problem, since it contains substances capable of increasing heat production and oxygen consumption for more than 20 minutes after the pepper is eaten.

Red Pecan Crackers

*1 cup **pecans**, soaked overnight*
1 cup sun-dried tomatoes, soaked for
several hours
½ cup flax seed, soaked overnight
2 strips kelp, soaked for 5–10 minutes
½ small sweet onion, finely chopped
1 red bell pepper, minced
sea salt to taste
Season with a combination of flavorings,
such as thyme, cayenne pepper, and
coriander
2 cups water

Combine kelp, sun-dried tomatoes, flax seed, and water in a blender. Blend until smooth.

Transfer the mixture to a food processor and add pecans. Process on high until thoroughly mixed. Move the paste into a bowl and stir in onion, red bell pepper, sea salt, and seasonings to taste. Mix well with a spoon. Spread the mixture on 3 or 4 dehydrator sheets with a rubber spatula. Place in dehydrator at 105°F for 12 hours. In about 8 hours you might want to turn them up and remove the teflex sheet as they continue to dehydrate. When the crackers are crisp, remove from the dehydrator and cut into desired shapes.

PECANS

The pecan is native to America. The English term pecan comes from the Algonquin Indian word *paccan* or *pakan,* meaning "a nut so hard it had to be cracked with a stone." The Algonquins also referred to walnuts and hickory nuts as *paccans.* Despite that description, much of their popularity came from being easier to shell than other North American nuts. They can usually be cracked just by crushing them against each other in your hand. George Washington and Thomas Jefferson both grew them.

Pecans contain phytochemicals that offer antioxidant protection from many diseases, including heart disease, diabetes, and cancer. Because pecans contain mostly monounsaturated fatty acids, they are recommended for low-fat diets by the American Heart Association.

Pecans are sodium-free and contain nearly 20 different vitamins and minerals including iron, calcium, potassium, phosphorus, and vitamins A, B, and C. Pecans are high in zinc, which generates testosterone. Both men and women benefit from this hormone that is responsible for increasing sexual desire. Pecans should be soaked overnight before eating.

Kamut Chips

½ cup flax seed, soaked overnight
½ cup water
*1 cup **Kamut Wheat**®*
3 cups yellow squash, cut in chunks
1 sweet onion, minced
sea salt to taste
cayenne pepper to taste

Kamut Wheat® should be soaked overnight and then sprouted for 2 or 3 days.

Rinse the flax seed and place in a blender with water. Blend as finely as possible and transfer mixture to a food processor. Add sprouted Kamut Wheat® and squash. Process until well blended. Add onion, sea salt, pepper, and any other seasonings to taste. Process briefly to combine flavors. Using a spatula, spread the mixture onto dehydrator sheets in a ¼-inch layer. Dehydrate 8 to 10 hours, or until crispy. Cut into squares and enjoy. Great with guacamole.

KAMUT WHEAT®

Kamut Wheat® is the registered trademark of Kamut International, which markets products made with the grain. It is an ancient relative of durum wheat. It originated in ancient Egypt in the Tigris–Euphrates Valley. A small sample of the seeds was sent to Montana wheat farmers by a World War II airman who claimed to have found them in Egypt.

The Montana farmers, the Quinn family, researched and propagated the crop, coining the name "Kamut" from the Egyptian word for wheat and trademarking it for the sale of the grain.

The grain, which has humpbacked kernels, is larger than common wheat, has 40 percent more protein , and is higher in lipids, amino acids, vitamins, and minerals.

Kamut Wheat® has a buttery flavor that has not been corrupted by modern farming techniques designed to produce higher yields. It has a much milder flavor than other green wheat grasses.

Fewer people show allergic reactions to this grain than to ordinary wheat, which represents a huge health benefit for wheat-intolerant individuals.

Rye Crackers

*1 cup **rye**, soaked and sprouted*
6 dates, pits removed
2 apples, cut in chunks
½ cup orange juice
pinch of sea salt

Soak rye berries overnight and then sprout them for 2 to 3 days.

Combine sprouted rye and remaining ingredients in a food processor and blend well. Spread the mixture ¼-inch thick on a dehydrator sheet and dehydrate for 4 hours. Turn crackers over and remove teflex sheet. Continue dehydrating for approximately 4 hours, or until desired crispness is reached. It will be easier to cut them into the desired shape after waiting several hours until the rye sheets have absorbed some moisture from the air, making them more pliable.

RYE

Rye is a newcomer when it comes to diet and cultivation. It was first grown about 400 B.C. Until then, it showed up mostly as a weed in other grain fields. Its lowly station as a weed relegated rye to the diets of the poor, well below wheat and barley.

Rye looks like wheat but the grain is longer and slimmer. It may vary in color from yellow-brown to gray-green.

For women, rye seems to help relieve menopause symptoms and may prevent breast cancer, because rye is a source of lignin, which balances women's estrogen activity.

Rye is also a high fiber source. Fiber binds to toxins in the colon and, by eliminating them from the body, reduces the chance of colon cancer. This same process also removes bile, causing the body to generate more bile, a process that helps to lower cholesterol levels.

Sweet Cheese Baklava

*2 cups **oats**, soaked and sprouted*
½ cup flax seed
1 cup raw honey
½ cup water
2 cup walnuts, coarsely chopped
1 tablespoon cinnamon
2 cups macadamia cheese

Soak oats overnight and sprout for 2 days.

Grind flax seed in a coffee grinder or dry Vita-Mix container. In a blender or Vita-Mix combine ground flax seed, drained, sprouted oats, ½ cup raw honey, and a little water, and blend until creamy. Spread the mixture about ⅛-inch thick onto dehydrating tray with teflex sheet and dehydrate until dry on top, but still pliable. Turn the crackers over and remove teflex sheets. Dehydrate for another 3 hours.

In a separate bowl, toss walnuts with cinnamon. Stir in ½ cup raw honey.

To assemble baklava: Spread a ½-inch layer of the macadamia cheese over the oat crust. Evenly sprinkle one third of the walnut mixture on top of the macadamia cheese. Repeat the layering process until all of the walnut mixture and macadamia cheese are used. You should end up with an oat crust on top. There should be enough for 3 layers. Refrigerate before cutting into squares.

OATS

Oats are a hardy cereal grain that can grow in very poor soil conditions. Their distinctive flavor is the result of the roasting process. Although oats are hulled after roasting, the process does not strip away their bran or germ, allowing them to retain a concentrated source of fiber and nutrients. Oat groats are whole oats that are processed by removing only the outer hull. They are highly nutritious but very chewy and must be soaked for a long time.

Oats are credited with being able to stabilize blood sugar. They are an excellent source of selenium, which works with vitamin E to aid in numerous vital antioxidant functions. Any food rich in water-soluble fiber is a good addition to the diet.

It is very hard to find truly raw oats, because whole raw oats turn rancid very quickly, and most companies will "lightly steam" the oats after harvest, heating them up to 212°F. Thus, they do not qualify as a raw food. However, during the transitional diet this is acceptable.

One source for organic oats (raw, fresh, rolled) is *www.naturalzing.com*

These oats are cold-rolled in small batches using special equipment to retain nutrients and flavor.

Wheat Crackers

*2 cups **wheat** berries, soaked
   and sprouted
½ cup flax seed, soaked overnight
1 cup sun-dried tomatoes, soaked for
   several hours
1 cup water
sea salt to taste
1 stalk celery, finely chopped
1 medium red onion, finely chopped*

Soak wheat berries for 12 hours. Then sprout for 2 or 3 days.

Process flax seed, sun-dried tomatoes, and water in a Vita-Mix or a blender until a smooth puree is produced. (If Vita-Mix is used, transfer the mixture to a food processor.) Add sprouted wheat berries and sea salt and process into a dough. Transfer mixture to a bowl and stir in celery and onion. Spread the mixture ¼-inch thick on dehydrator sheets. Dehydrate overnight, cut into squares, and turn over. Remove teflex sheets and dehydrate for another 2 hours or until desired crispness is reached.

WHEAT

Whole grains — especially wheat — are good sources of disease-fighting antioxidants which help prevent colon cancer, and, possibly, diabetes and heart disease. Scientists originally thought that the fiber was responsible for wheat's cancer-fighting abilities, but they have now discovered that it is the presence of antioxidants, in addition to fiber, which helps prevent cancer.

The health benefits of wheat depend entirely on using select 100 percent whole wheat products so that the bran and the germ of the wheat remain intact. Processing wheat into flour causes it to lose more than half of its nutritional value.

Whole wheat is rich in vitamins B_1, B_2, B_3, E, folic acid, calcium, phosphorus, zinc, copper, iron, and fiber. It is also a good source of dietary fiber and manganese, (which makes it a source of magnesium, vitamins B_3, B_5, B_6, iron, and protein) along with small amounts of potassium and selenium.

Wheat berries can be bought in any health food store.

Swiss Chard Guacamole with Cucumber

3 leaves of Swiss chard greens (remove the stems and use for juicing)
2 avocados, sliced
3 dates, pitted
2 tablespoons lemon juice
1 tablespoon cumin
sea salt to taste
2 cloves garlic, minced
*½ medium **bell pepper**, finely chopped*

Place all of the ingredients except red bell pepper and garlic into a food processor and mix until smooth. Stir in garlic and bell pepper. Serve on cucumber logs.

BELL PEPPERS

Peppers are excellent sources of vitamin C and beta-carotene, two very powerful antioxidants. These antioxidants work together to effectively neutralize free radicals, which can travel through the body causing tremendous amounts of damage to cells.

Red peppers are one of the few foods that contain lycopene, a carotenoid whose consumption has been inversely correlated with prostate cancer and cancers of the cervix, bladder, and pancreas.

Sweet peppers appear to have a protective effect against cataracts, possibly due to their vitamin C and beta-carotene content. Bell peppers showed a risk reduction effect of 0.7 percent, leading researchers to conclude that peppers provide *significant* protection.

Sweet red peppers also supply the phytonutrients lutein and zeaxanthin, which have been found to protect against macular degeneration, the main cause of blindness in the elderly.

Peppers also contain vitamin B_6 and folic acid. These two B vitamins are very important for reducing high levels of homocysteine. High homocysteine levels have been shown to cause damage to blood vessels and are associated with a greatly increased risk of heart attack and stroke.

Raw Tofu

2 cups **soybeans,** *soaked and sprouted*
1 cup water
2 tablespoons lemon juice
2 cloves garlic, minced
2 tablespoons fresh parsley, finely chopped
sea salt to taste

Soak soybeans overnight. Drain and rinse well. Place soybeans in the refrigerator until sprouted.

Blend soybeans and water in a blender. Add lemon juice. Blend to a fine cream. Pour cream into a cheese bag. Hang the bag over the sink and let it drain and ferment at room temperature for 6–8 hours or until tofu coagulates. Transfer the mixture to a bowl and stir in the remaining ingredients. Refrigerate before serving.

Serve with crackers, or as a dip with carrots or celery sticks.

SOYBEANS

The delicious, slightly nut-flavored soybean has been cultivated in China for more than 13,000 years, but soy's culinary versatility and recognition of its exceptional health benefits are a relatively recent phenomenon in the West. Different varieties of this truly amazing legume are available throughout the year.

The soybean is the most widely grown and utilized legume in the world, and it is one of the most well-researched, health-promoting foods available today. Like other beans, soybeans grow in pods, featuring edible seeds. While we most often think of them as being green, the seeds can also be yellow, brown, or black.

Soy is loaded with high-quality protein, meaning that it holds the full complement of amino acids. The body needs 22 amino acids but can only make 14. We get the other eight from foods, and soy is the only plant food that provides them all.

Just one cup of soybeans provides 57.2 percent of the Daily Value (DV) for protein, with less than 300 calories and only 2.2 grams of saturated fat. In addition, soy protein tends to lower cholesterol levels, while protein from animal sources tends to raise them. In addition to healthy protein, some of soybeans' nutritional high points include a good deal of well-absorbed iron: there is 58.9 percent of the DV of iron in that cup of soybeans, plus 46.2 percent of the DV of nature's relaxant, magnesium; 22.9 percent of the DV of heart-protective vitamin E; 22.9 percent of the DV of essential Omega-3 fatty acids; and 17.5 percent of the DV of bone-building calcium.

Dehydrated Fruits

mangos
papayas
pineapple
apples
lemon juice

Cut mango, papaya, pineapple, and apples into thin slices. Soak the pieces in lemon juice for several hours. Dehydrate for about 10 hours or until dry.

PINEAPPLES

Columbus was introduced to pineapples when he landed on the Caribbean island of Guadeloupe during his second voyage to America, and he and his men became the first Europeans to enjoy this delectable fruit. Because the pineapple superficially resembles a huge pine cone, the Spaniards called it *piña de Indias* (Pine of the Indies) — *pineapple* in English.

Research on bromelain, an enzyme in pineapple, shows it to be anti-inflammatory and mucolytic, meaning that it has the capacity to take the red out of a fiery sore throat and eliminate mucus. Fresh pineapple is rich in bromelain, a group of sulfur-containing proteolytic (protein-digesting) enzymes that not only aid digestion but have also been used experimentally as an anti-cancer agent.

Pineapple is an excellent source of the trace mineral manganese, which is an essential cofactor in a number of enzymes important in energy production and antioxidant defenses. For example, the key oxidative enzyme *superoxide dismutase*, which disarms free radicals produced within the mitochondria (the energy production factories within our cells), requires manganese.

Just one cup of fresh pineapple supplies 128 percent of the DV of this very important trace mineral. In addition to manganese, pineapple is a very good source of thiamin and a good source of riboflavin, two B vitamins that are cofactors in enzymatic reactions central to energy production.

Crunchy Nuts and Seeds

2 cups water
2 teaspoons sea salt
a handful of almonds, sunflower seeds,
   and **quinoa**

Combine water and sea salt. Soak nuts and seeds in this solution for several hours or overnight, then dehydrate until dry.

QUINOA

Quinoa (KEEN-wah), which grows from ten- to twenty-thousand feet above sea level, was an important source of food for the Indian tribes native to the Andes Mountains of Peru and Bolivia.

Quinoa was first cultivated more than 5,000 years ago with corn and potatoes as one of the three foods considered the centerpiece of the Andean diet. Quinoa was a primary food source, with animal foods largely secondary. Archeological evidence indicates that, like most grains, wild quinoa plants have smaller seeds than domesticated plants.

Quinoa contains more protein than any other grain. Unlike most grains, quinoa is not deficient in the amino acid lysine. Because it contains a larger quantity of lysine, it is considered to contain all the essential amino acids, making it a complete protein. Quinoa also has more calcium, fat, iron, phosphorus, and B vitamins than many other grains.

You can purchase organic quinoa from Country Life Natural Foods at *www.clnf.org,* or by phone at 1-800-456-7694.

Cookies &
Other Treats

Energy Bars

2 cups filberts
10 Medjool dates, pitted
1 cup coconut meat
1 tablespoon cinnamon
3 tablespoons lemon juice
½ cup whole raisins or currants
½ cup walnuts, coarsely crushed
½ cup shredded unsweetened coconut

Grind filberts in a coffee grinder or Vita-Mix.

Combine ground filberts, dates, coconut meat, cinnamon, and lemon juice in a food processor and puree. Transfer the mixture to a bowl. Add raisins and walnuts and mix with a spoon. Press into a rectangular pan and refrigerate. Cut into 1-inch thick bars. Roll in shredded coconut before serving.

FILBERTS/HAZELNUTS

The filbert is a type of hazelnut that got its name because it ripens near the feast of St. Philbert, a seventh-century monk. The terms "filbert" and "hazelnut" are used interchangeably. These nuts are native to North America, Asia, and Europe. They still grow wild across the northern part of the U.S.

The flavor is mild. Eaten with green vegetables, they are a wonderful body-building food. Filberts are high in essential vitamins, minerals, fiber, and protein. They are rich in calcium and trace minerals. They are one of the best nut sources for monounsaturated fats. Several medical studies have shown that hazelnuts lower the risk of heart disease because their fat content is primarily monounsaturated.

Hazelnuts are also rich in antioxidants such as vitamin E and selenium, which appear to reduce the risk for cardiovascular disease and certain cancers.

Hazelnuts may have an impact on the production of the drug Taxol, an anticancer drug, because they contain *paclitaxal*. Previously the only source of this substance was the Pacific yew tree. These trees are slow-growing, in limited supply, and it takes several trees to make even a small amount of Taxol.

*I order my filberts from **www.clnf.com.***

Healthy Heavenly Halva

2 cups raw tahini
2 cups pine nuts, soaked for several hours
½ cup raw honey
2 tablespoons lemon juice
4 tablespoons **coconut oil**
1 cup coconut water
1 tablespoon vanilla
⅓ cup carob

Place tahini, pine nuts, honey, lemon juice, coconut oil, and vanilla in a food processor. Mix until a doughy consistency is reached, adding coconut water only as needed. In a glass, mix carob with a little coconut water until all carob is absorbed. Fold carob mixture into halva dough slowly to get a marbled effect. Press into a square or rectangular pan and spread evenly. Refrigerate for several hours. The mixture will thicken as it cools. Cut into wedges before serving.

COCONUT OIL

Coconut oil is a stable vegetable oil. It can be kept at room temperature for a year and will show no evidence of rancidity.

Coconut oil contains a healthy form of saturated fat that can actually help with weight loss. It contains no dangerous trans-fats that even olive oil has. Trans-fats raise LDLs or "bad" cholesterol levels, which can lead to clogged arteries, heart disease, type-II diabetes, and other degenerative conditions.

According to Dr. Bruce Fife, author of the best-selling book *The Healing Miracles of Coconut Oil,* this oil is not only one of the good fats that our body needs, but it may perhaps be the most healthy of them all! If you are still cooking your food you should definitely consider using coconut oil for all your sautéing and baking needs.

Dr. Fife explains the healing powers of coconut oil. Clinical studies have shown that coconut oil has anti-microbial and anti-viral properties. It can kill certain bacteria; combat viral, fungal, and yeast infections; and improve digestion and nutrient absorption. It helps to heal ulcers and other stomach and intestinal disorders, lowers cholesterol, and helps prevent heart disease. It can help those with diabetes, chronic fatigue, and thyroid problems. Coconut oil improves metabolic processes in the body and helps you to achieve optimal weight. It boosts your energy level.

According to another book, *Coconut Oil For Health and Beauty* by Cynthia and Laura Holzapfel, coconut oil is an invaluable beauty aid. It not only prevents wrinkling of the skin, and protects against the free radical damage that causes aging, but also effectively rejuvenates your skin. It is also attributed to be helpful in fighting acne.

Most coconut oil sold in America is refined. Look for organic, unrefined, cold-pressed, extra-virgin coconut oil, which retains all of its healthy qualities.

*I buy coconut oil from **www.rawfood.com.***

Cream Sandwich Cookies

2 cups almonds, soaked overnight
2 cups dried shredded coconut,
  unsweetened
½ cup raw carob
*½ cup raw **honey***
1 cup raw cashews, soaked overnight

Place almonds, 1 cup shredded coconut, carob, and ¼ cup raw honey in the food processor. Process until smooth. Spoon the batter into cookies 2 inches in diameter and ¼-inch thick on the teflex sheets and dehydrate for 4 hours.

Remove teflex sheets, turn cookies over, and dehydrate for an additional 4 hours.

Filling: Mix cashews with remaining cup of coconut and raw honey in a food processor. Put filling between two cookies and refrigerate before serving.

HONEY

For 5,000 years, honey has been considered one the purest, most natural remedies for a wide range of ailments and complaints.

Honey is the answer to treating your sweet tooth. Besides being sweet, research indicates that honey offers many of the same benefits as fresh fruits and vegetables.

The darkest honey contains antioxidant levels similar to spinach and garlic and is much tastier. Honey is an effective energy source that does not encourage hypoglycemia.

The University of Memphis found that using honey as a carbohydrate source improved performance and power during exercise. Researchers concluded that honey might be a good pre-workout energy source because it does not spike blood sugar and insulin levels. Another study suggests that combining honey with a protein supplement may boost post-workout recuperation.

Be sure that the raw honey you purchase is truly raw and has not been processed or heated. My husband is from a family with several generations of beekeepers. He tells me that fresh honey is only liquid for about a month or so after it is removed from the hive, then it crystallizes. Be sure that raw, organic honey is not liquid because, if it is, it has been heated to maintain a liquid consistency.

A good source for raw, unheated, unprocessed honey is *www.goldminenaturalfood.com*, or call 1-800-475-3663.

Buckwheat Banana Cookies

*2 cups **buckwheat**, soaked and sprouted*
2 bananas, peeled and sliced into rounds
½ cup flax seed, soaked overnight
½ cup raw honey
1 tablespoon vanilla
1 tablespoon cinnamon
juice of ½ small organic lemon

Soak buckwheat for at least 6 hours and sprout for 2 days.

Combine sprouted buckwheat, flax seed, honey, vanilla, and cinnamon in a food processor and puree. Add a little lemon juice to help the dough to turn over. Using a cookie dough scoop, place balls of the mixture on the mesh dehydrating sheets. Press them flat. Place a slice of banana on top of each cookie and dehydrate for 24 hours.

BUCKWHEAT

Buckwheat seems to have originated in China as early as the 10th century. It came to Europe and Russia in the 14th and 15th centuries, and to America through the Dutch colonists in the 17th century.

Buckwheat is not a cereal grain; rather it is a fruit — kin to rhubarb. The name may have come from the Dutch *bockweit* (meaning "beech wheat") — a reference to its nutlike shape and wheat-like characteristics. The flowers are fragrant and used by bees to make a particularly strong-flavored dark honey.

Buckwheat produces quercitin, an antihistamine that prevents the release of chemicals that cause allergic symptoms. It alleviates these symptoms without causing drowsiness or nervousness like most commercial medications.

It contains a good supply of flavonoids that extend the benefits of vitamin C and act as antioxidants, lowering the risk of heart disease and cholesterol. Magnesium, important for lowering blood pressure, is also present in buckwheat. Researchers believe that buckwheat is capable of controlling blood sugar, thereby lowering the risk of diabetes.

Banana-Raisin Cookies

1 cup pistachios, soaked overnight
4 pitted Medjool dates
2 tablespoons orange juice
*2 **bananas**, peeled and cut in chunks*
½ cup raisins

Combine pistachios, dates, orange juice, and bananas in a food processor. Transfer mixture to a bowl and stir in raisins. Spread mixture on dehydrator teflex sheets in ⅓-inch layers. Dehydrate for 6 hours. Flip the cookie crust over and remove teflex sheets. Dehydrate for another 6 hours. Cut into desired shapes and enjoy!

BANANAS

Bananas probably originated in Malaysia some 4,000 years ago. The army of Alexander the Great found them in India as early as 327 B.C. Arabian traders took them to Africa, where the Portuguese discovered them in the 15th century. Bananas appeared in seacoast towns of the United States in the 19th century. Until refrigeration was available, they could not be transported inland.

Dr. Douglas N. Graham, author of *Nutrition and Athletic Performance* and a consultant to professional athletes, considers bananas to be one of the world's finest foods for providing energy. The carbohydrates in bananas are of both simple and complex forms. The complex carbohydrate yields its fuel slowly, thus providing a lasting energy source.

He believes that "there is no fruit which will encourage the muscles to refuel themselves more rapidly than bananas." For athletes, his recommendation is ten to fifteen bananas per day. Dr. Graham is so enthusiastic about bananas that each time I re-read his book I start including more bananas in my diet; however, I never was able to eat more than two per day.

Bananas are rich in potassium, which aids in cardiovascular health and helps to promote bone health. Potassium may counteract the increased urinary calcium loss caused by the unusually high salt content in the American diet. Slowing calcium loss can slow the rate that bones thin and weaken.

Bananas can replenish the body's stores of potassium, one of the most important electrolytes, which helps regulate heart function as well as fluid balance after a bout of diarrhea.

Bananas contains vitamin C, one of the strongest defenses against many forms of cancer, including lung, pancreatic, cervical, breast, bladder, and stomach. They provide about two grams of cholesterol-reducing fiber. Bananas are nearly perfect. Try to buy organic in the health food stores and eat them only when there are covered with dark spots, an indication that they are fully ripe.

Cashew-Carob Cups

1½ cups filberts, soaked overnight
8 Medjool dates, pitted
¼ cup raw **carob**
1½ cups raw cashews, soaked overnight
½ cup coconut flakes
3 tablespoons raw honey
juice of ½ small organic lemon
standard paper muffin cups

Mock Chocolate Crust: Combine filberts, dates, and carob in a food processor. Process until dough forms a ball. Use a muffin pan with paper liners. Fill each cup half full, pressing the dough down.

Filling: Place cashews, coconut flakes, honey, and lemon juice in blender and mix on high until smooth. Finish filling cups with this mixture. Place in the freezer for a half an hour, than remove the cake cups from the forms and keep refrigerated, uncovered, overnight or until ready to serve. Makes an elegant dessert.

CAROB

According to Greek records from 4 B.C., carob was called the Egyptian fig. Its sticky properties were used to seal the wrappings on mummies. Romans ate the green pods, enjoying their natural sweetness. It has been cultivated for 4,000 years. The Moors introduced it into Spain along with citrus fruits and olives.

Carob is actually a legume. Both the seeds and pods are edible. The seeds are ground into a flour for use as a cocoa substitute. Although carob tastes somewhat similar to chocolate, it has one-third the calories, no caffeine, and, unlike chocolate, is almost completely fat-free and nonallergenic. Carob is 80 percent protein and contains vitamins A, B_1, B_2, B_3, and D. It is also high in calcium, phosphorus, potassium, and magnesium, and contains iron, manganese, barium, copper, and nickel. It is ideal for building strong bones.

The carob that is sold in most health food stores looks like a fine powder and is roasted. A good source for raw carob is *www.rawfood.com*. Their carob is harvested from wild-growing carob-pod trees in Spain. It looks like semi-coarse powder and is produced by utilizing unique grinding process that uses a high-speed "hammer grinder." The temperature does not exceed 100°F.

Almond Cookies with Raisins

1 cup almonds, soaked overnight
2 bananas
½ cup shredded coconut
juice of 1 small lemon
*1 cup **raisins***

Combine all ingredients except raisins in a food processor. Add a little lemon juice to help the dough turn, and puree. Transfer the mixture to a bowl and stir in raisins. Use a cookie dough spoon to place balls of dough onto dehydrator teflex sheets. With a spatula, flatten the dough into a round-shaped cookie about ¼-inch thick. Dehydrate for 6 hours. Turn cookies over, remove the teflex sheets, and dehydrate for 2 more hours or until desired consistency is reached.

RAISINS

Drying grapes into raisins has been practiced since ancient times. Raisins were produced in Persia and Egypt as early as 2000 B.C. One of the first references to them is in the Old Testament. Romans prized raisins so highly that they were used to decorate sacred sites. They were also used as currency, and as rewards at sporting events. The ancient Romans spread the practice of drying grapes into raisins throughout the Empire and, from there it spread throughout the world.

Like other dried fruit, raisins are a concentrated source of calories, sugar, and nutrients. They supply dietary fiber (both soluble and insoluble), as well as some iron, potassium, and B vitamins. The type of fiber found in raisins has been shown to be helpful in lowering high cholesterol levels, reducing the risk of colon cancer, and alleviating some of the uncomfortable symptoms of irritable bowel syndrome

Raisins are a good source of potassium, which helps build strong bones. Potassium has also been shown to lower high blood pressure and reduce the risk of heart disease. In fact, diets high in potassium-rich foods are associated with a reduced incidence of heart attack.

Raisins also contain vitamin B_6 and dietary fiber. Vitamin B_6 helps prevent atherosclerosis by assisting in the conversion of homocysteine, a molecule that can damage blood vessel walls, into other, benign substances.

Raisins are a good source of the nutrient iron — essential for raw food eaters. It assists enzymes in the production of amino acids, hormones, and neurotransmitters, and is a major component of hemoglobin, which helps carry oxygen in red blood cells.

Mango Pistachio Cookies

2 cups pistachio nuts, soaked for 4 hours
  and peeled
¼ cup raw honey
1 teaspoon coconut oil
*2 cups **mango**, peeled and sliced*
1 cup walnuts, coarsely crushed

Use food processor to mix pistachio nuts, honey, coconut oil, and slices of mango together. Transfer the mixture into a bowl and stir in crushed walnuts. Mix with a spoon. Form the dough into cookie shapes on a lightly oiled mesh dehydrator sheet and dehydrate for 12 hours.

MANGOES

Mangoes, native to Malaysia and India, have been culti-vated for at least 4,000 years. Mango trees blossom and bear fruit in regions where there is a good rainfall for four months, followed by dry weather.

Mangoes are very nutritious and provide an excellent source of carotene. The total carotenoids in mango increase with the stage of ripening. Eating mangoes in season may store enough vitamin A in the liver to last for the rest of the year. Vitamin A is highly beneficial for the prevention of defi-cient disorders like night blindness.

In fact, a study shows that mangoes may have better cancer-fighting ability than apples or bananas. "We think man-goes have some unique antioxidants as well as quantities of antioxidants that might not be found in other fruits and veg-etables," said nutrition and immunity specialist, Susan Percival, of the UF Institute of Food and Agricultural Sciences, which conducted the study.

Antioxidants inhibit cancer formation by protecting cells against damage from free radicals, oxygen atoms that have lost an electron and become unstable. "When a cell is dam-aged, it can become cancerous," Percival said. "We can't say these compounds from mangoes are going to prevent cancer in humans, because those studies haven't been done. But what we can say about the mango is that it contains potent antioxidants, and it would be a good part of a healthy diet."

Check for smaller mangos in Asian stores. I like them better.

Dream Ice Cream

3 rounded teaspoons tahini
1 avocado, pitted
6 Medjool **dates,** *pitted*
4 rounded teaspoons raw carob
1 cup coconut water

Combine all ingredients in Vita-Mix or regular blender and blend well. Transfer to bowl and freeze for 2 or 3 hours before serving. Scoop Dream Ice Cream into individual glasses. You will have to convince yourself that it is not a traditional ice cream.

DATES

Dates are definitely the "crown of sweets," an ideal food which is easy to digest. According to Islamic tradition, *Sayyidah Mariam* (the Virgin Mary) mother of *Pbuh* (Jesus) had dates as her food when she felt labor pains and during her confinement.

Experiments have shown that dates contain stimulants that strengthen the muscles of the uterus in the last months of pregnancy. This helps the dilation of the cervix at the time of delivery on one hand and reduces bleeding after delivery on the other.

Dieticians consider dates as the best food for women in confinement and those who are breast-feeding. Dates contain elements that assist in alleviating depression in mothers and that enrich breastmilk with all of the elements needed to make a child healthy and resistant to disease.

Some dietary institutes recommend dates for children suffering from hyperactivity. Modern science has also proved the effectiveness of dates, in preventing diseases of the respiratory system. Dates are effective against night-blindness.

Within half an hour of eating dates, the body is re-energized. A shortage of sugar in the blood is usually why people feel hungry. The nutritional qualities of just a few dates will alleviate the feeling of hunger. After breaking a fast with dates, the body does not require as much food, helping to avoid excessive eating.

Orange-Banana Bread

1 cup wheat berries, sprouted
1 banana, cut in chunks
8 Medjool Dates, pitted
*½ of an **orange**, peeled, separated in*
  sections and de-seeded
½ inch ginger root, shredded

Soak 2 cups of wheat berries overnight and sprout for two days.

Combine all ingredients in a food processor and puree until smooth. On a dehydrator sheet, form the dough into a loaf about 1½ inches tall. Dehydrate for 13 to 15 hours. When you take the loaf out of the dehydrator, it should be crisp on the outside and moist on the inside.

ORANGES

Oranges originated thousands of years ago in southern China. From there they found their way to India. Traders introduced them into Europe by the early 15th century, Columbus introduced them to the Caribbean on his second voyage, proving that they were considered an important food source.

Vitamin C in oranges is well known for boosting immunity, fighting colds, and helping to eliminate exercise-induced free radicals that cause soreness. Organic oranges have up to 30 percent more vitamin C than conventional oranges, even though they are half the size. The nitrogen in fertilizers used to grow conventional oranges may cause the fruit to absorb more water. Researchers theorize that the extra water means more vitamin C moves into the peel.

Owing to the multitude of vitamin C's health benefits, it is not surprising that research has shown that consumption of vegetables and fruits high in this nutrient is associated with a reduced risk of death from all causes, including heart disease, stroke and cancer.

The health benefits of oranges also include fiber. One orange has 15 percent of the recommended daily value. Fiber is known to reduce high cholesterol levels. Therefore, I eat whole oranges instead of juicing them. For some people, orange juice, with its powerful cleansing effect, can cause a toothache in crowned teeth; however, eating whole oranges does not normally create this discomfort.

Raw Pies,
Cakes & Tortes

Banana-Nut Pie

2 tablespoons lemon juice
2 cups pine nuts, soaked for several hours
1 cup coconut meat
2 bananas
6 Medjool dates, pits removed
3 rounded teaspoons raw carob
*3 tablespoons whole **psyllium powder***

Combine lemon juice, pine nuts, coconut meat, one sliced banana, dates, and carob in a Vita-Mix or food processor fitted with an "S" blade. Stir in psyllium powder. Transfer mixture into a 9-inch pie pan and smooth the top with a rubber spatula. Place in the freezer for at least 2 hours, or until ready to serve. Before serving, cut the second banana into very thin slices and arrange on top of pie.

WHOLE PSYLLIUM POWDER

Psyllium, also called *fleawort* or *flea seed husk,* is grown in India. Arabian and Persian merchants began transporting it as early as the 10th century A.D.

As early as the mid-19th century, psyllium was used throughout the United States and Europe as a mild laxative. It is still widely used, especially in homeopathic medicine and specialized food disciplines, although there are now synthetic compounds.

Psyllium is used as an emollient and laxative and in the treatment of chronic constipation and diarrhea. It is effective because it contain dense mucilage which naturally swells into a gelatinous mass on contact with liquid. Psyllium is an excellent, calorie-free source of soluble dietary fiber.

Because psyllium is high in fiber and mucilage, it helps regulate bowel function, and promotes healthy cleansing of the large intestine, expelling toxins as it does its work. Its health benefits may include minimizing constipation, intestinal inflammation, ulcers, and irritable bowel syndrome. Research indicates that it also helps control some aspects of atherosclerosis, diabetes, hemorrhoids, and cholesterol levels.

Layered Apple Pie

Lemon-Macadamia "Ricotta"
2 cups macadamia cheese
2 tablespoon lemon juice
pinch of sea salt

Place all ingredients in a blender and pulse a few times until thoroughly combined. Add a little water as needed and pulse until the texture becomes fluffy. Place in a bowl, cover, and set aside.

Savory Cranberry Sauce
½ cup raw honey
4 tablespoons lemon juice
½ cup cranberries
1 tablespoon whole psyllium powder

Mix all ingredients in a blender. Place in a bowl, cover, and set aside.

Crust
½ cup flax seed
*1½ cups **almonds,** soaked*
10 Medjool dates, soaked for a few hours
and pitted

Grind flax seed in a coffee grinder or dry Vita-Mix. Combine all ingredients in a food processor and process until dough forms a ball. Press the mixture into a 9-inch glass pie plate. Store in the freezer until ready to fill.

Pie
3 medium Granny Smith apples
3 tablespoons walnuts, coarsely crushed
3 tablespoons cinnamon
whole mint leaves to garnish

Cut apples in half. Using a mandoline, shave apples into very thin slices. Line the bottom of the crust with two layers of apple slices. Spread one-third of the Savory Cranberry Sauce over it, and top with one-third of ricotta. Sprinkle with cinnamon and crushed walnuts, using 1 tablespoon of each. Add another two layers of apples and repeat layers of the Savory Cranberry Sauce, ricotta, cinnamon, and crushed walnuts twice more. Garnish with mint leaves.

ALMONDS

Almonds are a member of the same family as the rose, plum, cherry, and peach. The difference is that the juicy fruit with a hard pit is replaced by a leather-like covering over nut meat. The almond tree is native to Asia and North Africa.

Almonds and almond oil were known in Greece and Italy long before the Christian era. The tree is mentioned in the Bible as being one of the best fruit trees in Canaan. The rod of Aaron was an almond branch, and the almond is one of the symbols on the tabernacle candlestick. Jews still carry almond blossom rods to the synagogue on festival days.

The Romans were probably responsible for the almond's introduction to Britain, where it appears on Anglo-Saxon lists of plants. By the 16th century, it was grown in England primarily for its blossoms.

Almonds are high in protein and have no cholesterol. Almonds contain vitamin E, a powerful antioxidant with cancer-fighting qualities. They contain more magnesium than spinach. Almonds provide phosphorus, which is good for bones and teeth. They also have potassium, iron, zinc, copper, manganese, and trace amounts of the B vitamins thiamin and riboflavin.

Almonds are higher in calcium than any other nut. Research has indicated that almonds can lower cholesterol levels. Unblanched almonds have almost double the fiber when compared to blanched. Almonds are high in folic acid, which is important for reducing birth defects.

Clever Carrot Cake

7 carrots
1 cup almonds, soaked overnight
*1½ cups **walnuts***
½ cup flax seed, soaked overnight
1 cup shredded coconut
1 cup raisins
3 tablespoons whole psyllium powder
1 teaspoon vanilla
1 cup raw honey
natural waxed paper

Process carrots, almonds, 1 cup of walnuts, and flax seed through Champion Juicer using the solid plate, or process in a food processor. Transfer mixture to a large bowl. Stir in shredded coconut, raisins, psyllium powder, vanilla, and honey, and mix well with a spoon. Cut a long strip of natural waxed paper 2 inches wide and apply along the wall of springform pan. Press mixture firmly into 10-inch springform pan. Refrigerate for two hours.

Icing
1 cup raw cashews, soaked overnight
1 cup raw honey
juice of ½ lemon
1 teaspoon vanilla

Blend cashews, honey, lemon juice, and vanilla in Vita-Mix until mixture is thick and creamy. Unmold cake from springform pan and place on a serving platter. Ice top and sides of cake and garnish with walnuts. Using a sharp knife or vegetable peeler, peel a carrot into spiral strips and make several cones for decoration (see photo in back).

WALNUTS

There is no better way to add extra nutrition, flavor, and crunch to a meal than by adding walnuts. Walnuts are harvested in December but are available all year.

Even a small amount of walnuts has a beneficial effect in lowering total cholesterol and low-density cholesterol levels. Walnuts contain an essential amino acid that helps hypertension by keeping the inner walls of blood vessels smooth and allowing blood vessels to relax.

Walnuts are called brain food, partly because of their brain-like appearance, but also because of a high concentration of Omega-3 fats. The brain is more than 60 percent structural fat. Cell membranes are the gatekeepers of the cell. Anything that wants to get into or out of a cell must pass through the cell's outer membrane. Omega-3 fatty acids, which are especially fluid and flexible, make this process a whole lot easier. For the brain cells to function properly, the brain's structural fat needs are primarily the Omega-3 fatty acids found in walnuts and flax seed.

Walnuts are also high in antioxidants and contain magnesium, potassium, and vitamins E and B_6.

*Try eating black walnuts, which are far superior in nutritional value. I buy them from **www.clnf.com**. I soak them and eat with my morning juice. Because of their specific taste, they do not work well in recipes.*

Macadamia Cheese Cake

Crust
1 cup filberts, soaked overnight
1 cup walnuts
10 dates, pitted
5 rounded tablespoons raw carob
juice of ½ small organic lemon

Combine all ingredients in a food processor and process until dough forms into a ball. Press the dough into a 8-inch pie pan and refrigerate, uncovered, overnight (or freeze for several hours).

Filling
3 cups macadamia cheese
3 young **coconuts** *(meat only)*
1 teaspoon coconut oil
½ cup raw honey
½ cup coconut water, as needed

Combine macadamia cheese, coconut meat, coconut oil, raw honey, and coconut water in a blender or Vita-Mix. Blend on high until thick and creamy. Pour into crust and refrigerate several hours before serving.

COCONUTS

This fruit of the coconut palm tree provides both solid and liquid food. Coconuts have been a part of the Southeast Asian diet for thousands of years. Indigenous peoples who have eaten unrefined coconut products as a major part of their diet for centuries are traditionally healthy and trim with thick, shiny hair and flawless skin.

The hairy, brown coconuts sold in grocery stores or shown in movies like *Castaway,* starring Tom Hanks, are old coconuts. A young coconut is a coconut which has had the outer shell partially removed; it usually looks like a cylinder with a point on top. Coconuts in their early stages of growth are the most health enhancing. Young coconuts have medicinal qualities for heart, liver, and kidney disorders.

Coconut meat is rich in essential fatty acids. In a coconut palm, water from the soil travels up through many fibers, being filtered and purified in the process. When it is stored in the coconut itself, it is sterile. Coconut water is close in composition to human blood plasma and one of the highest sources of electrolytes. It has been reported that many people's lives were saved during World War II in Third World countries by coconut IVs. Coconut water is also rich in calcium and trace minerals, and can be used to re-mineralize the body.

The biggest trick to eating a young coconut is opening it. There are several techniques for opening young coconuts. As always, practice makes perfect. I normally shave the cone surface with a sharp knife and then whack it several times with a meat cleaver about 2 inches from the top until the top comes off or the opening is big enough to pour the liquid through. At first, try to make a small opening, just large enough for a straw. Drink coconut water immediately after opening the coconut. Once exposed to air and light, the liquid rapidly loses most of its nutrients and begins to ferment.

Young coconuts are usually found in Asian markets or Mexican markets. For further information on coconuts and on how to find young coconuts in your area, check *www.youngcoconuts.com.*

Durian Dream Pie

Crust
½ cup flax seed
1½ cup walnuts
10 Medjool dates, pits removed
juice of ½ small organic lemon

Grind flax seed in a coffee grinder or dry Vita-Mix. In a food processor, combine walnuts, ground flax seed and dates, with lemon juice and vanilla. Process until dough forms a ball. Press the dough into 9-inch glass pie plate. Refrigerate overnight or place in the freezer for a couple of hours.

Filling
½ **durian** (meat)
2 coconuts (meat only)
3 tablespoons raw tahini
juice of ½ small organic lemon
3 tablespoons mesquite pod meal
2 tablespoons vanilla

Combine all ingredients in a food processor and puree until a creamy mixture is formed. Pour into the crust and smooth the surface with a spatula. Refrigerate several hours before serving.

DURIAN

Durian is grown in Thailand and Malaysia, where it is prized. The durian is a tall tree towering as high as 40 meters in the jungle rainforest or in semi-orchard. Seed trees may take 8 to 10 years to bear fruit. A grafted durian tree grows to 15–20 meters tall.

In the Western world, durian is available in Asian markets in most cities. The name, comes from the Indonesian word which means "thorny." The size of a soccer ball and covered with spikes, it can be lethal if thrown.

The fruit is green to brown in color, pendulous, round or oblong in shape, and completely covered with strong, sharp thorns. It is a capsule which splits into five parts when ripe, and each segment contains brown seeds covered with thick, firm, creamy, yellow pulp with an overpowering aroma.

Some people think it smells like rotten cheese, but it tastes like vanilla custard. According to a popular saying, durians smell like hell and taste like heaven. The smell is so horrific that it is banned from public consumption in Singapore where the fruit is very popular. There are "No Durian" signs in the subway — the standard red circle with a slash through the silhouette of a spiky fruit.

The durian is rich in essential fatty acids and high quality protein, and is reputed to be an aphrodisiac. Many think that eating a durian is one of the most intense of all food experiences.

Durian is a high-calorie fruit. A whole durian is 900 to 1000 calories. Durian is particularly rich in fat, 34 to 36 percent.

You must taste it at least once! I like it very much, even though I do not eat it more than once a year.

Pumpkin Pie

Pie Crust

1 cup walnuts, soaked overnight
1 cup raw pumpkin seeds, soaked
overnight
10 Medjool dates, pits removed
2 tablespoons lemon juice

Place ½ cup pumpkin seeds on dehydrator sheet. Dehydrate for several hours, or until crunchy. Combine walnuts, remaining pumpkin seeds, dates, and lemon juice in the food processor. Process until the dough forms a ball. Place dehydrated pumpkin seeds on the bottom of 9-inch glass pie plate. Press the dough into the pan. Refrigerate overnight or place in the freezer for a couple of hours.

Filling

*4 cups raw **pumpkin**, peeled and*
cut in chunks
1 avocado
½ cup fresh squeezed carrot juice
1 cup raw pine nuts, soaked for
several hours
½ teaspoon ginger powder
1 teaspoon vanilla powder
½ cup raw honey

Place pumpkin, avocado, carrot juice, pine nuts, ginger, vanilla, and honey into a blender or Vita-Mix. Blend until smooth. Spread the mixture evenly on the crust, smooth the surface with a spatula and refrigerate several hours before serving.

PUMPKINS

Native Americans used pumpkin flesh and seeds for food and medicine. They used the seeds to treat intestinal infections and a variety of kidney problems. The flowers were used topically on cuts and abrasions.

Pumpkin rarely appears in the average American diet except as pie at Thanksgiving. In other places, such as Japan and South America, pumpkins are used in a variety of main dishes.

Considering that contemporary dietary theories call for more beta-carotene, high fiber, and low fat and cholesterol, pumpkin should be a more substantial part of our diet. Pumpkins are a tasty source of vitamins and minerals, particularly beta-carotene, vitamin C, and potassium. They also have fiber, magnesium, and folic acid.

Not only is pumpkin flesh a tasty addition to your diet, but pumpkin seeds are one of the most flavorful and nutritious seeds around. They have a sweet, nutty taste and a chewy texture.

Recent studies have encouraged eating pumpkin and pumpkin seeds as an anti-inflammatory for arthritis and as a deterrent to prostate problems in men because pumpkin seeds are a good source of zinc, which protects the prostate by helping to reduce prostate size.

Dr. Pratt, author of the book *Superfoods Rx,* said, "The best food on the planet to get alpha carotene, beta-carotene in its most bio-available form, is pumpkin."

Fabulous Fruitcake

2 cups filberts
*1 cup **brazil nuts***
1 cup flax seed
20 Medjool dates
1 cup raw carob
juice of 1 lemon
2 cups coconut water or as needed
½ cup dried currants
2 cups dehydrated mango, pineapple,
*   apple, banana, papaya, diced*
½ cup pecans, coarsely crushed
6 teaspoons raw honey
additional pecans, walnuts, and dried
*   fruits for decoration*

Grind filberts, brazil nuts, and flax seed separately in a coffee grinder or dry Vita-Mix. Set aside in separate containers.

Combine dates, carob, lemon juice, and coconut water in a blender or Vita-Mix. Blend well. Pour the mixture into large bowl. Add ground filberts, brazil nuts, and flax seed one ingredient at a time, mixing well after each addition. Stir in dried fruits and pecans and mix well with hands until coated. Press the mixture into a bundt cake pan coated with coconut oil. Place in the freezer for an hour or two. Remove cake from pan. Place on a cake plate and glaze with a thin coat of raw honey. Decorate with whole pecans, walnuts, and dried fruits. Refrigerate for at least 8 hours before cutting.

BRAZIL NUTS

Brazil nuts grow wild in the jungles of South America. Purchased Brazil nuts probably come from wild trees because, unlike many nuts, they are not grown on plantations. The wild trees are huge evergreens with trunks up to six feet in diameter; they can grow up to 150 feet tall.

Brazil nuts add some $44 million annually to South American economies because they are the only food in the global economy that is found almost exclusively in remote natural forests rather than on cultivated land. The *castañeros,* those who make their living collecting the nuts in the wild, come into contact with vipers and jaguars, diseases, and armed territorial skirmishes.

The nuts have a pleasing, rich flavor, and are one of the richest nuts in fat. Always buy them in the shell because commercially removing the shell requires boiling.

Because of their high fat content, Brazil nuts are good for energy. Brazil nuts are the food richest in selenium, an antioxidant linked to low rates of cancer and heart disease. Just one Brazil nut a day is enough to maintain daily selenium amounts.

Chocolate Sheet Cake

*⅓ cup **cacao beans***
1 cup pistachios, soaked for several hours
*   and peeled*
½ cup un-soaked walnuts
10 Medjool dates, pitted
juice of ½ small orange
a pinch of sea salt
2 tablespoons buckwheat,
*   soaked overnight*

Using a coffee grinder or Vita-Mix, grind the cacao beans to a fine powder. In a food processor combine pistachios, walnuts, dates, cacao powder, orange juice, and sea salt. Process until mixture forms a uniform batter. Remove batter from food processor and smooth onto teflex sheets about ¾-inch high. Sprinkle with buckwheat kernels. Dehydrate for 8 to 10 hours.

CACAO BEANS

Chocoholics rejoice! The cacao bean is the source of all chocolate and it can be eaten raw. More importantly, cacao in its natural state is highly nutritious. Most of its nutrition is destroyed when it is cooked. Cacao is the seed from the fruit of an Amazonian tree. The beans were used as money by the Mayans and Aztecs.

The actual beans contain no sugar. The fat content varies from 12 percent to 50 percent depending on growing conditions and species. No research validates cacao beans as a source of weight gain. The fact that cacao contains more magnesium than any other food source may explain why women crave it during their menstrual periods. Magnesium has the ability to balance brain chemistry, which tends to go awry every 28 days. Magnesium builds strong bones, and is often deficient in American diets.

Small amounts of the stimulant caffeine are present in raw beans but show no negative effects. Over-stimulation seems to become strong only when cacao beans are cooked. Raw and unroasted, there are no such side effects from the beans.

Women may also subconsciously crave chocolate because cacao beans have rare inhibitors that increase circulation of serotonin and other neurotransmitters in the brain, which may assist in maintaining and renewing youthful qualities. Never underestimate a woman's instincts.

In the recipes you can use cacao beans with their skins on.

*One day I was giving a food preparation demonstration and used cacao beans abundantly in my recipe. The next day, two women told me that they could not fall asleep that night. That is when I learned that you **can** have too much of a good thing. Consume no more than three or four cacao beans at one time.*

Blueberry Pie

2 cups walnuts
10 Medjool dates, pitted
*1 cup **blueberries**, frozen*
1 teaspoon vanilla

Combine all ingredients in a food processor and mix well until dough forms a ball.

Transfer the dough into desired container and freeze for several hours before serving.

BLUEBERRIES

Originally called star berries by Native Americans because of the star-shaped calyx on top, blueberries are one of only three fruits (including cranberries and grapes) native to North America. Blueberries contain fiber, vitamins, minerals, and antioxidants.

When researchers discovered that blueberries were a major source of antioxidant phytonutrients, the berries became nutritionally important. The U.S. Department of Agriculture (USDA) ranks blueberries first in antioxidant activity compared to forty other fruits and vegetables. Other healthy qualities have been identified in blueberries. The deep bluish-purple skin contains anthocyanins, the flavonoid pigments responsible for its antioxidant properties. These stimulate enzymes that protect against cancer as well as slowing tumor growth.

Blueberries also contain two additional cancer-inhibiting compounds, ellagic acid and resveratrol. According to researchers, pro-anthocyanidins and tannins, found in blueberries and cranberries, promote urinary tract health by blocking or preventing the growth of bacteria. They may be useful in fighting heart disease and cancer.

Researchers at Tufts University have discovered that blueberries reverse short-term memory loss in aged rats. If the fruit proves to have the same effect on humans, life could be greatly improved by adding one or two cups of blueberries to your daily diet.

They are sweet enough to satisfy cravings for dessert, yet low in calories. Common companions include blackberries, cherries, cranberries, purple grapes, raspberries, and strawberries.

Carob-Currant Fudge

½ cup walnuts
1½ cups pine nuts, soaked for
    several hours
1 cup **currants**
5 rounded teaspoons raw carob
1 tablespoon coconut oil
2 tablespoons lemon juice
½ cup pecans, coarsely crushed, for
    decoration

Combine all ingredients except pecans in a food processor. Mix well until a dough of uniform consistency is formed. Remove mixture from processor and press into 8-inch glass square dish. Smooth the top with a rubber spatula. Sprinkle with crushed pecans. Refrigerate for at least 2 hours to allow fudge to become firm. Cut into squares and serve.

CURRANTS

Currant is probably a corruption of the Greek city Corinth, which shipped small raisins (dried Black Corinth grapes) throughout Europe. Currants, which are about one quarter the size of raisins, are seedless and very dark.

Currants may be part of the custom of trick-or-treat which is thought to derive from a European custom called "souling." Beggars asked for "soul cakes," square pieces of bread with currants. The beggars promised to say prayers for the departed of those who gave them the cakes. The more cakes they were given, the more prayers they would say to ease the deceased's passage from limbo to heaven.

Currants contain vitamin A, thiamin (B_1), riboflavin (B_2), niacin, vitamin C, calcium, phosphorus, iron, and potassium in large enough amounts to be considered a highly desirable food.

Like other dried fruit, currants supply a healthy amount of both soluble and insoluble dietary fiber. The type of fiber found in currants has been shown to be helpful in lowering high cholesterol levels, reducing the risk of colon cancer, and alleviating some of the uncomfortable symptoms of irritable bowel syndrome

The potassium in currants may counteract the increased urinary calcium loss caused by the high-salt diet typical of most Americans. Potassium has also been shown to lower high blood pressure and reduce the risk of heart disease. In fact, diets high in potassium-rich foods are associated with a reduced incidence of heart attack.

Shakes, Sorbets & Soufflés

Fantastic Figs Shake

5 fresh figs
2 tablespoons raw tahini
¼ cup raw carob
2 cups filtered water

Place all ingredients in a blender or Vita-Mix and blend on high. Transfer to two tall glasses and refrigerate before serving.

No dessert was ever so delicious and nutritious at the same time!

FIGS

The best food that can be taken by those who are brought low by long sickness and are on the way to recovery. They increase the strength of young people, preserve the elderly in better health and make them look younger with fewer wrinkles. — Pliny, Roman historian (A.D. 62–113)

Figs are among the ancient fruits native to Western Asia and the Mediterranean. They were highly valued by both the Egyptians and the Greeks. As is so often the case in history, Solon, the ruler of Attica (639–559 B.C.), issued a decree to reserve their use for the Greeks, making it illegal to export them.

Figs have the highest sugar content of any common fruit. A dried fig is about 50 percent sugar, but it also contains protein and abundant calcium, magnesium, phosphorus, and potassium.

Figs are a good source of the indigestible food fiber lignin, a protein-breaking enzyme. Figs also contain ficin, another protein-breaking enzyme, similar to papain. Ficin also has some laxative effects, so the combination of lignin and ficin makes figs a very efficient laxative.

In some cultures, like Greece, stuffed fig leaves are a popular menu item. Fig leaves consistently show anti-diabetic properties and can actually reduce the amount of insulin needed by persons with diabetes.

Tamarind-Tahini Twirl

*1 cup **tamarind** juice*
2 teaspoons raw tahini
1 banana, cut in chunks and frozen
3 rounded teaspoons raw carob
1 cup filtered water

To make tamarind juice, soak tamarind, fresh or dried, in warm water (1 part pulp to 3 parts water). Soak for a few minutes to soften. Stir and mash it with a fork to help it dissolve. Then strain it through a fine sieve. Repeat with a little more water if there is still undissolved pulp left in the sieve. Discard pulp and seeds, and use juice as needed.

Combine all ingredients in Vita-Mix or regular blender and blend well. Pour into two glasses and chill before serving.

TAMARIND

The tamarind is grown as a shade and fruit tree in all tropical and subtropical areas, including South Florida. The fruits look like irregularly curved and bulging pods of beans. Inside is a sticky flesh that tastes similar to dates but with a sweet, sour taste and fruity aroma. Tamarind is a legume with large brown seedpods. It is also known as the Indian date. Tamarind juice, compressed tamarind, and tamarind concentrate are used in Indian, Thai, Caribbean, and Latin American cooking.

Tamarind pods are delicious if eaten raw. Remove the crisp pod and fibrous threads and enjoy the flesh, discarding the hard stones as you eat. The pulp is sold in block form or as a paste and is available at Indian grocery stores.

Tamarind is known to cool the system and cleanse the blood. The pulp, rich in vitamins and minerals, is used in Chinese medicine. It increases appetite. Tamarind is antiseptic, a mild laxative, and a digestive aid. It is high in calcium, phosphorus, carotene, and magnesium.

Plum Pudding

*4 ripe **plums**, pitted*
1 avocado, pitted
4 Medjool dates, pitted
3 rounded teaspoons raw carob
1 cup filtered water

Blend all ingredients in a blender or Vita-Mix until smooth and creamy. Add water as needed for desired consistency. Refrigerate and serve. Makes a light, delectable "chocolate" pudding.

PLUMS

When fresh, this fruit is a plum; when dried, it is a called a prune. Substances found in plum and prune are classified as phenols, and their function as antioxidants has been well-documented.

These damage-preventing substances are particularly effective in neutralizing a particularly destructive oxygen radical called *superoxide anion radical,* and they have also been shown to help prevent oxygen-based damage to the fats that comprise a major portion of our brain cells or neurons, the cholesterol and triglycerides circulating in our bloodstream, and the fats that make up our cell membranes.

Plum and prune consumption increases the absorption of the vitamin C content of this fruit. In addition to assisting with absorption of iron, vitamin C helps make healthy tissue and bolsters the immune system.

Plums are a laxative and a bowel stimulant. Plums are a good source of potassium, vitamin A, vitamin E, and the minerals copper and iron. They are considered to be good for the circulation and help combat fluid retention.

Mesquite Velvet Mousse

*½ cup raw **mesquite pod meal***
1 coconut (meat and water)
1 cup cashews, soaked overnight
2 tablespoons raw honey

Mix all ingredients in a blender or Vita-Mix until smooth and serve immediately.

MESQUITE POD MEAL

For 2,000 years, mesquite was a source of nutrition for Native Americans and indigenous peoples throughout arid regions worldwide. Mesquite trees thrive in desert regions that are unsuitable for agriculture. The pods are harvested and ground into meal.

Mesquite flour has a sweet, slightly nutty flavor with a hint of molasses. Mesquite is a good source of calcium, magnesium, potassium, iron, and zinc. Mesquite is low in carbohydrates and fat.

Mesquite was an important source of food for Native Americans in the Southwest and Mexico. The move from the nomadic life sustained by mesquite meal to a more sedentary life without mesquite meal is believed to be one of the primary causes of the increased incidence of obesity and diabetes in Native Americans.

Diabetes is growing in the general U.S. population, too. Mesquite is important in a diet because it works to balance blood sugar. The natural sweetness in mesquite pods comes from fructose, which does not require insulin to be metabolized. The high dietary fiber causes nutrients to be absorbed slowly, which prevents spikes in blood sugar. Maintaining a constant blood sugar level over a longer time period suppresses hunger.

Peach-Pineapple Sorbet

*1 cup frozen **peaches**, cut in chunks*
1 banana, cut in chunks and frozen
1 cup pineapple, peeled, diced, and frozen
1 cup pine nuts, soaked for several hours

Alternate frozen mango slices with banana and 2 tablespoons of pine nuts while processing through a Champion Juicer using the solid blank. Combine the mixture in a bowl and stir with a spoon. Serve immediately.

PEACHES

Peaches go back to the 10th century B.C. in China, where they appear in the art of the time. A Chinese bride was referred to as a peach. The Greek philosopher Theophrastus gave the peach its name in about 300 B.C. He thought it came from Persia and named it for that country.

In the first century A.D. the Romans began cultivation. Peaches spread throughout Europe and to the Americas. Early settlers planted them with such regularity that, by the early 18th century, it was thought to be native to the Americas.

Peaches contain vitamins A, B, and C, as well as calcium, fiber, and potassium. Like all yellow/orange fruits and vegetables, they contain quantities of beta-carotene known for building immune system resistance to the damage of free radicals and lowering the risk of skin cancer.

Peaches have diuretic properties. They act as a natural laxative and produce strong cleansing effects on the body, especially the kidney and bladder. They push toxins out of the body and, as a result, improve complexion and hair.

Lemon-Papaya Soufflé

½ cup ground flax seed
2 cups papaya, diced
3 tablespoons raw honey
juice of ½ small organic **lemon**

Grind the flax seed in a coffee grinder. Transfer the ground flax seed to a blender and combine with the other ingredients. Puree until smooth. Pour into small glasses and refrigerate before serving.

LEMONS

Lemons, a cross between the lime and the citron, are thought to have originated in China or India, where they have been cultivated for some 2,500 years. Arabs brought them to Spain in the 11th century. The Crusaders introduced lemons to Europe, and Columbus brought them to the New World.

Lemons are filled with vitamin C, which is vital to the function of a strong immune system. The immune system's main goal is to protect you from illness, so a little extra vitamin C may be useful in conditions like colds, flus, and recurrent ear infections.

Vitamin C is also one of the main antioxidants found in food. Vitamin C neutralizes free radicals in the body, both inside and outside of the cells. Because free radicals can damage blood vessels and can change cholesterol to make it more likely to build up in artery walls, vitamin C can be helpful for preventing the development and progression of atherosclerosis and diabetic heart disease. It is also considered an effective deterrent to macular degeneration.

Lemons, due to their cleansing and detoxification properties, act as solvents and mucus-dissolvers in the body.

Tangerine-Mango Mix

2 **tangerines,** *peeled, sectioned,*
and seeded
1 banana, cut in chunks and frozen
1 mango, diced and frozen
1 teaspoon raw honey

Combine all ingredients in a blender or Vita-Mix. Puree until smooth. Serve immediately.

TANGERINES

Tangerines are delicious citrus fruits that are sweeter and less acidic than oranges. Tangerines also peel more easily. They contain many of the same health benefits as oranges.

They are rich in vitamin C and other healthy vitamins and antioxidants like all orange-colored fruits.

Tangerines also contain two chemicals that seem to inhibit the growth of breast cancer cells in test tubes. Depending on the type of breast cancer cell, the tangerine chemicals can be more powerful at inhibiting growth than the chemical found in soy-based foods that has previously shown promise as an inhibitor. Fruit chemicals are more powerful when interacting with current breast cancer treatments.

Researchers at the Centre for Human Nutrition at the University of Western Ontario intend to continue their work in animal studies and, if successful, plan human trials.

I can say that tangerines are my favorite fruit.

Cranberry Sauce

*2 cups **cranberries**, fresh or frozen*
2 apples, cut in chunks
½ cup walnuts, soaked overnight
½ cup raw honey

Combine all ingredients in a food processor or Vita-Mix and puree. Serve immediately.

CRANBERRIES

Cranberries, a native of North America, were called "crane berries" because cranes were inordinately fond of them. They were a staple of the Native American diet as an ingredient of pemmican — preserved, dried meat. Berries were pounded into the meat, along with suet.

No one is quite sure how cranberries became a holiday staple, but it was probably the simple fact of their being in season late in the year. Being bright and nearly indestructible, they were not only eaten but also strung on thread to decorate the house and tree at Christmas.

Cranberries contain vitamin C and potassium in good quantities with low calories. Cranberries have traditionally been used to treat urinary tract and vaginal infections. Recent research has indicated that the remedy is not just a home remedy. Cranberries may also promote gastrointestinal and oral health, as well as lowering low-density lipoprotein (LDL) and raising good cholesterol. They are considered an aid in stroke recovery and may even help prevent cancer.

Grapefruit Sorbet

1 cup freshly squeezed red
   grapefruit *juice*
1 cup macadamia nuts, soaked overnight
½ cup coconut water
meat of 1 coconut
½ cup raw honey

Mix all ingredients in Vita-Mix. Place mixture in an ice cream machine and follow manufacturer's directions for making ice cream.

Alternative method: Simply freeze for an hour or two before serving.

GRAPEFRUIT

The grapefruit, not even 300 years old, is the baby on the fruit block. It seems to have appeared as a horticultural accident during the 1700s in Jamaica. The grapefruit may be a cross between a pummelo and an orange. Pummelo, a native of Malaysia and Indonesia, seems to be the grapefruit's father. It is about the size of an orange.

In Jamaica, grapefruit is not popular because of its bitter, acidic taste. The grapefruit came to the U.S. in 1823. In 1870, John A. MacDonald noticed an unusual tree near his home in Orange County, Florida. He bought all of the fruit and, soon after, established the first grapefruit nursery.

Studies indicate that fresh grapefruit daily may help keep the arteries clear of cholesterol plaque. Researchers at the University of Florida in Gainesville report that about three tablespoons of grapefruit pectin a day can lower blood-cholesterol levels.

The rich pink and red colors of grapefruit are due to lycopene, a carotenoid phytochemical. Lycopene appears to have anti-tumor activity. Phytochemicals in grapefruit called limonoids inhibit tumor formation, and the enzyme produced causes a reaction in the liver that helps to make toxic compounds more water-soluble so that the body can eliminate them more easily.

Grapefruit can have a negative reaction with some drugs, so be sure to check with your pharmacist or doctor before including it in your diet.

Raspberry Pudding

*2 cups **raspberries***
1 cup almonds, soaked overnight
2 tablespoons raw honey
½ cup filtered water

Place raspberries, almonds, and honey in a blender or Vita-Mix, with a small amount of water and mix until smooth. Pour into individual serving bowls.

RASPBERRIES

Raspberries probably came from Asia Minor. Roman records have been found, dating raspberries back to the 4th century A.D. Like so many other fruits and vegetables, the Roman Empire probably spread the cultivation. The English were responsible for actually cultivating and improving raspberries during the Middle Ages.

The plants were exported to the U.S. by the late 1700s, although the black raspberry is indigenous to North America. Red raspberries were considered to have more cachet, so their American cousins were not cultivated for another hundred years.

Black raspberries are rich in antioxidants. Researchers have found that they contained nearly 40 percent more antioxidants than blueberries or strawberries. As an antioxidant food containing ellagic acid, raspberries help prevent unwanted damage to cell membranes and other structures in the body.

Raspberries are an excellent source of manganese and vitamin C — two critical antioxidant nutrients that help protect the body's tissue from oxygen-related damage. They contain riboflavin, folate, niacin, pantothenic acid, and vitamin B_6. Raspberries are also high in dietary fiber.

Smoothies

Supreme Strawberry Slush

2 oranges, peeled
⅓ inch ginger root
2 cups fresh organic **strawberries**
4 ice cubes

Juice oranges and ginger. Combine strawberries with orange and ginger juice in a blender or Vita-Mix and puree until smooth. Serve immediately.

STRAWBERRIES

Doubtless God could have made a better berry, but doubtless God never did. — William Butler, 16th century Englishman, on the subject of strawberries

Cultivated since ancient Rome, strawberries have retained their popularity throughout the centuries. One species or another has been cultivated throughout Europe, Russia, South America, and the United States.

Its original name was "strewberry," from the way the berries lay among the leaves as though tossed there by the handful. It gradually changed to the present "strawberry," possibly because they were sometimes mulched with straw, making it look as though they were growing from the straw.

The ellagitannin content of strawberries has actually been associated with decreased rates of cancer death. In one study, strawberries topped a list of eight foods most linked to lower rates of cancer deaths among a group of 1,271 elderly people in New Jersey. Those eating the most strawberries were three times less likely to develop cancer compared to those eating few or no strawberries.

In animal studies, researchers have found that strawberries help protect the brain from oxidative stress and may reduce the effects of age-related related declines in brain function. Researchers found that feeding aging rats strawberry-rich diets significantly improved both their learning capacity and motor skills.

Strawberries, like other berries, are famous in the phytonutrient world as a rich source of phenols. In the strawberry, these phenols are led by the anthocyanins (especially anthocyanin 2) and by the ellagitannins. The anthocyanins in strawberry not only provide its red color, they also serve as potent antioxidants that have repeatedly been shown to help protect cell structures in the body and to prevent oxygen damage in all of the body's organ systems.

Apricot-Apple Ambrosia

4 fresh **apricots**, pitted and cut in chunks
2 Golden Delicious apples, cored and
  cut in chunks
1 cup filtered water
1 tablespoon raw honey

Combine all ingredients in a blender or Vita-Mix and puree until smooth. Chill before serving.

APRICOTS

Apricots originated in China, coming to Europe by way of Armenia. Spanish missionaries planted them in Southern California missions in the late 18th century. The climate was perfect and most are still grown there.

The flavor is sweet with a tartness that is more pronounced when the fruit is dried. Apricots, like all orange-colored fruits and vegetables, are high in beta-carotene, which helps lower cholesterol and protects against optical deterioration. Apricots also contain vitamin A, which is important in preventing free radical damage in vision-related diseases such as macular degeneration.

Apricots are a good source of fiber. Fiber is important in preventing constipation and digestive conditions such as diverticulosis. The fruit is also a good source of potassium, which prevents leg cramps.

When purchasing dried apricots, be sure they are unsulfured. Drying processes that use sulfur can cause allergic reactions. Apricots dried without sulfur will be brown instead of orange, but they are much healthier.

Airy Amber Blend

*2 cups **cantaloupe**, cut in chunks*
1 cup pineapple, cut in chunks
1 peeled banana, cut in chunks
1 tablespoon grated lemon zest
4 ice cubes

Juice cantaloupe. Pour cantaloupe juice into blender or Vita-Mix. Add pineapples, banana, lemon zest, and ice cubes and puree. Serve immediately.

CANTALOUPES

Cantaloupe is actually a muskmelon. No one seems quite sure when the ridged, netted muskmelon became known as cantaloupe in the States, but it has been within the last 50 years. No one is quite sure where it originated either: Persia, Afghanistan, or Armenia. What *is* known is that melons are a part of antiquity. They are mentioned in the ancient Sumerian epic, *Gilgamesh,* and in the Bible.

Originally the size of oranges, cantaloupes were re-introduced into Italy centuries after the fall of Rome. Through cultivation, they grew larger and attained their present size. Although popular in the rest of the world, they obtained wide acceptance in the United States only after the Civil War.

Cantaloupe, being orange, is an excellent source of vitamin A because of its concentrated beta-carotene content. One cup of cantaloupe provides 129 percent of the daily value for vitamin A. Both vitamin A and beta-carotene are important vision nutrients. Beta-carotene has also been the subject of extensive research in relationship to cancer prevention and prevention of oxygen-based damage to cells.

Cantaloupe is a good source of vitamin B_6 and potassium, as well as dietary fiber, folate, vitamin B_3, vitamin B_5 and vitamin B_1. The combination of all these B-complex vitamins, along with the fiber found in cantaloupes, makes them an exceptionally good fruit for supporting energy production through good carbohydrate metabolism and blood sugar stability. These B-complex vitamins are required in our cells for processing carbohydrates (including sugars), and cantaloupe's fiber helps ensure that cantaloupe's sugars are delivered into the bloodstream gradually, keeping the blood sugar on an even keel.

Persimmon-Papaya Smoothie

3 medium **persimmons,** *peeled and*
  cut into chunks
1 cup papaya, peeled and cut in chunks
2 tablespoons raw honey
juice of 1 lemon
½ tablespoon cinnamon

Combine all ingredients in blender or Vita-Mix with a small amount of water and liquefy until smooth. Pour into individual glasses and chill before serving.

PERSIMMONS

Persimmons originated in China and are beginning to gain more popularity in America. They resemble orange-colored cherry tomatoes and must be eaten when they are as soft as an overripe tomato. Otherwise they are extremely astringent and will dry out your mouth very quickly. If you eat the unripe fruit, you'll find it has a bitter, furry taste. That's because persimmons are rich in tannins, excellent antioxidants also found in red wine and tea.

As well as being very tasty, persimmons are highly nutritious. They're a good source of vitamin C and one of the richest sources of beta-carotene. Persimmons contain high concentrations of minerals and phenolic compounds — all instrumental in fighting atherosclerosis, a leading cause of heart disease, heart attacks, and stroke.

Persimmons contain twice as much dietary fiber as apples. They tend to have mild laxative properties. The peel has higher fiber levels than the pulp. Persimmons also contain more of the major phenolics (antioxidants) than apples. Besides being high in fiber, they contain no fat.

The best thing about persimmons is that they have a unique flavor. You can just eat them fresh. When ripe, they are very sweet, much like jam. You can buy persimmons unripe, and let them ripen at room temperature. To hasten the process, place them in a paper bag in a warm, dark place.

Ponceau Pomegranate Punch

1 pomegranate
juice of 1 medium orange
½ inch ginger root
1 tablespoon raw honey

Squeeze a pomegranate in your hands until the seeds inside release their juice. (Much as you do an orange to make it juicier.) Place the pomegranate in a small plastic bag while squeezing it to avoid getting splashed if the skin breaks open. When the pomegranate feels very soft, make a small cut and squeeze the juice into a container. Put through a strainer to remove the seeds or their pieces. Make orange and ginger root juice in a juicing machine. Combine juices and add honey. Chill before serving.

POMEGRANATES

Bursting with seeds, the pomegranate has long been a symbol of fertility, hope, beauty, and prosperity. Legend has it that human beings become immortal by eating its seeds. In Greek mythology, Persephone was so tempted by the luscious fruit while she was captive in the Underworld that she ate six seeds, destining the earth to six months of winter every year while she stayed below.

The fruit's name means "seeded apple." Some religious scholars believe that a pomegranate was the true forbidden fruit in the story of Adam and Eve, as apples were not native to the Mesopotamian region, where Eden might have been.

It contains substantial fiber plus vitamin C, most of the B vitamins, copper, pantothenic acid, magnesium, and phosphorus. One pomegranate contains more potassium than 1½ navel oranges.

In the past, pomegranates were used as astringents, to remove tapeworms, and for inflammation and diarrhea. In a small Israeli study, healthy volunteers who drank two ounces of pomegranate juice daily for two weeks showed a significant decrease in lipid oxidation, a contributing factor to plaque buildup in arteries.

In a Korean study, polyphenols extracted from pomegranates inhibited estrogen formation, possibly protecting against breast cancer. Pomegranate juice has three times the antioxidant activity of either red wine or green tea.

Kiwi-Strawberry Nectar

*3 **kiwis**, cut in chunks*
1 cup fresh organic strawberries
1 tablespoon raw honey
1 cup coconut water

Combine ingredients in a blender or Vita-Mix and puree. Serve immediately.

KIWIS

Kiwifruit originated in the Chang Kiang Valley of China where the Khans thought of it as a great delicacy. An English collector for the Royal Horticultural Society of Britain obtained samples, and it was introduced into Western culture during the mid 1800s.

Kiwis are actually berries. The black seeds, a starburst against its green flesh, store most of the vitamins and fiber. The fuzzy skin of kiwis should be eaten for maximum benefit.

Kiwis are becoming almost as popular as apples and bananas. Kiwis contain as much potassium as bananas — an important mineral for active people because it helps eliminate leg cramps.

Kiwi is also a good source of two of the most important fat-soluble antioxidants, vitamin E and vitamin A. Vitamin A is provided in the form of beta-carotene. This combination of both fat- and water-soluble antioxidants makes kiwi able to provide free radical protection on all fronts.

In phytonutrient research, kiwi is recognized for its ability to protect DNA (in the nucleus of human cells) from oxygen-related damage. Because kiwi contains a variety of flavonoids and carotenoids that have demonstrated antioxidant activity, these phytonutrients in kiwi may be responsible for this DNA protection.

The fiber in kiwifruit has also been shown to be useful for a number of conditions. Researchers have found that diets that contain plenty of fiber can reduce high cholesterol levels, which may reduce the risk of heart disease and heart attack. Fiber is also good for binding and removing toxins from the colon.

Cherubic Cherry Cocktail

*2 cups dark sweet **cherries**, pitted*
2 cups coconut water
½ teaspoon powdered ginger

Combine the cherries with all other ingredients in a blender or Vita-Mix and puree. Serve immediately.

CHERRIES

Loveliest of trees, the cherry now
Is hung with bloom upon the bough... — A.E. Housman

The beauty of the cherry tree in bloom is probably more famous than the nutritious elements of its fruit. The Japanese have long used the cherry blossom in all phases of their art, including the Samurai sword, where it was the emblem of war and destiny. Many kimonos were decorated with it, as it also symbolizes happiness.

The cherry probably originated in the Orient and was spread westward by birds. Cherries were found in Greece and Rome. The Moors are thought to have introduced them into Spain.

Cherries contain phytochemicals that may lower the risk of cancer, heart disease, and other chronic diseases. Both sweet and tart cherries are rich in antioxidants, including anthocyanins, catechins, chlorogenic acid, flavonal glycosides, and melatonin. Anthocyanins extracted from cherries have shown to contain anti-inflammatory properties, through inhibition of cyclooxygenase (COX) activities and scavenging of the reactive nitric oxide (NO) radical.

Russel Reiter, Ph.D., a researcher at the University of Texas Health Science Center at San Antonio, who has been studying melatonin for years, has found that cherries — especially tart cherries — are incredibly rich in the hormone, which affects sleep patterns and has been promoted as an anti-aging supplement.

Eating sour (tart) cherries may be as beneficial for the heart and circulatory system as a source of vitamin E, an antioxidant. Researchers at Michigan State University found that anthocyanins, giving cherries their deep color, inhibit free radicals that contribute to heart disease, cancer, and degenerative conditions caused by aging.

The researchers' findings, published in the *Journal of Natural Products* and the *Journal of Agriculture and Food Chemistry* in 1999, show that sour cherries are not only powerful antioxidants but also contain anti-inflammatory properties.

Garnet Grape Geneva

*2 cups red seedless **grapes***
1 cup strawberries
1 cup coconut water
1 tablespoon vanilla
4 ice cubes

Puree strawberries, grapes, and coconut water in blender on high speed. With machine running, add one ice cube at a time until mixture is thick and smooth. Serve immediately.

GRAPES

Grapes have been a part of history for so long that both the Greeks and Romans had gods dedicated to them, along with accompanying festivals. As fermentation has long been part of the culture of grapes, the festivals had a reputation for being Bacchanalian.

Red and purple grapes are excellent sources of anthocyanin phenols, as are most berries, plums, currants, and other deep red-blue fruits. The only commonly eaten foods other than grapes that are known to contain resveratrol are peanuts and possibly mulberries. But the amounts do not compare favorably to grapes.

Grapes contain beneficial compounds called flavonoids, which are phytochemicals that give a vibrant purple color to grapes, grape juice, and red wine; the stronger the color, the higher the concentration of flavonoids.

Additionally, researchers have found that phenolic compounds in grape skins inhibit protein tyrosine kinases, a group of enzymes that play a key role in cell regulation. Compounds that inhibit these enzymes also suppress the production of a protein that causes blood vessels to constrict, thus reducing the flow of oxygen to the heart.

However, to receive benefits comparable to those gained from drinking a glass of red wine, you need to drink more grape juice. A recent study found that six glasses of grape juice produced the same beneficial effect as two glasses of red wine, without the harmful effects of alcohol.

Mouthwatering Watermelon Whirl

4 cups ripe **watermelon**
2 cups fresh pineapple juice
2 tablespoons raw honey
½ teaspoon powdered ginger
mint leaves to garnish

Cut watermelon into chunks and remove seeds. Put in freezer for 2 hours or until frozen.

Place frozen watermelon in blender. Add honey, ginger, and pineapple juice. Process until very smooth. Pour into tall stemmed glasses and garnish with mint leaves. Chill before serving.

WATERMELONS

Originating in Africa, watermelons were first cultivated in Egypt, where they are recorded in hieroglyphics. The fruit was even placed in the tombs of many Egyptian kings. It is not surprising that watermelon played such an important role along the Nile and in other countries where water is in short supply. Watermelon can always be counted on as a thirst-quencher.

Watermelon is a good source of lycopene, a red-tinted carotenoid that may help prevent prostate cancer. Watermelon meets the American Heart Association's criteria for a heart-healthy food. It also counteracts the inflammation that contributes to conditions like asthma, athero-sclerosis, diabetes, colon cancer, and arthritis. Watermelon is an excellent source of vitamin C and of vitamin A, notably through its concentration of beta-carotene.

Watermelon is rich in the B vitamins necessary for energy production. It a very good source of vitamin B_1, vitamin B_6, vitamin B_5, biotin (another B vitamin), as well as magnesium, potassium, and dietary fiber. Watermelon has a high nutrient density which makes it easy to get its healthy nutrients; it also has a higher water content and lower calorie content than almost any other fruit. At only 48 calories per cup, watermelon offers a strong vitamin kick for its quantity.

Watermelon is best eaten by itself. But for those of you who absolutely must have a recipe, here is one. Watermelon makes a delicious drink and ginger gives it a sharp, spicy flavor. It is a mouthwatering combination.

Pear-Parsley Swirl

*3 ripe juicy **pears***
2 cups parsley (leaves and stems) loosely
*   packed*
2 cup filtered water

Puree pears, parsley, and filtered water in blender on high speed. With machine running, add one ice cube at a time until mixture is thick and smooth. Serve immediately.

This recipe is contributed by Victoria Boutenko, raw food lifestyle author and founder of *www.rawfamily.com*. She promotes drinking green smoothies. Green smoothies are blended drinks made of approximately 60 percent ripe organic fruit mix with 40 percent organic green leafy vegetables. These smoothies look emerald green but have a dominant fruit flavor. This is the most delicious way to get your daily intake of greens.

PEARS

The perfect pear is said to be a work of art, and indeed this luscious, sensually shaped fruit has been the subject of much artwork. Greek writings dating back to 300 B.C. testify to the reverence pears have inspired. Louis XIV was particularly fond of pears in 17th century France. The response to pears in 19th century New England was so overwhelming that it was called "pearmania."

The pear is a member of the rose family. The sweetness of pears can be attributed to levulose, the sweetest of the natural sugars. In the U.S., fresh pears are available year-round, with each variety having its own peak season. The most popular pear in the U.S. is the Bartlett, also used for canned pears. Bartletts are yellow or red, and feature the classic pear shape. D'Anjou pears are green or red and oval-shaped with smooth skin. Boscs are long-necked with rough brown skin. But most favored by connoisseurs is the large, round, and extra juicy Comice.

Few fruits match the fiber of a pear. A medium pear boasts four grams, almost half of which is pectin, a soluble fiber that helps control blood cholesterol and blood sugar. Pears also contain vitamin C (10 percent daily value) and potassium (208 milligrams), all for 98 calories.

Although not well-documented in scientific research, pears are often recommended by healthcare practitioners as a hypoallergenic fruit that is less likely to produce an adverse response than other fruits.

Advanced Raw Food Lifestyle

In this book, I have tried to explain the meaning behind the raw food diet, to present beauty as a powerful motivator, and to introduce recipes that will ease the transition. It is remarkably easy to follow the raw food lifestyle, but the real challenge is the switch. The recipes presented in this book have helped in my transition as I was trying to free myself of the craving for cooked food; I hope they will do the same for you!

In the beginning, because of your past training, your resolve will swing like a pendulum. You will constantly worry about whether or not you are getting enough nutrients. Should I eat more fruits? More greens? More nuts? The only way you will rid yourself of these fears is by gaining your *own* quantifiable firsthand experience. When this happens you will not be enduring the raw food diet, you will be enjoying the truth. Balance is the key!

Not all raw foods are created equal! Some are healthier for you than others. Certain ingredients are essential to the transition but should be gradually eliminated once the change is complete. While on the raw food diet, do not force any dietary changes. Let your body be your guide.

For example, mushrooms are excellent for filling the initial void left by eliminating cooked food, but exercise moderation in eating them. Listen to your body; you will know when it is time to give them up.

Raw soy recipes are certainly better than tofu or processed soymilk. There is nothing wrong in making raw tofu from sprouted soybeans during the transition phase, but as you progress, all soy dishes should be avoided because even "organic" soybean crops are now genetically modified (GMO). Dishes involving marinating in Nama Shoyu are very helpful when you miss heavily flavored cooked food. However, in preparation of this sauce, the soybeans are boiled and, although fermentation makes soy products into a somewhat digestible food, it is still cooked and salted.

Raw cakes, pies, and cookies were indispensable in my battles with sugar cravings. I relied heavily on them in the beginning but find that I am making fewer and fewer desserts for myself. When I do, I use coconut water as the main sweetener. Dried fruits are not the healthiest of foods, but they were crucial during my transitional phase. They will help you eliminate such foods as processed cookies, chips, pastries, etc. All of the dishes involving dried fruits must be eaten in great moderation. (You should always brush your teeth after eating, but absolutely do it after eating dried fruits.)

Another tremendous stumbling block for me was giving up bread. During the transition, I did use some grains. I have included several recipes that helped me over that particular hurdle. Again, in time, grain dishes will become too heavy for your digestive system. The same applies to sprouted beans. Give them up for good as soon as you can. It will bring you to another level of health.

If you have a serious health challenge you should exclude grains, beans, mushrooms, soy products, and dried fruits entirely from your diet. However, for most of us, the success rate will be much higher if we start with a variety of transitioning raw food dishes and then gradually simplify as we ascend to the basics: vegetable juices, simple greens plus vegetable salads, soaked nuts and seeds, seaweed, and some fruits.

It is not unusual for a long-time raw food eater to have only one or two meals per day.

Even my own regimen has changed since the interview I gave to *Get Fresh!* magazine. These days my first meal is at 11:00 A.M. I have green vegetable juice and a handful of soaked nuts. My second (and last) meal is at 2:00 P.M. I usually have a medium bowl of salad with different vegetables. Baby greens, tomatoes, cucumbers, kohlrabi, cabbage, strips of dry dulse, and tahini dressing are among my favorite staples. Occasionally, I eat a piece of fruit or a cup of berries, but I feel my best with just two meals and no snacking. Two meals serve me very well and give me a lot of energy.

If you have not read my first book, *Your Right to Be Beautiful,* you will probably have many questions after you finish reading this book. I recommend reading *Your Right to Be Beautiful* even before you begin transitioning with *Beautiful on Raw.* In *Your Right to Be Beautiful,* I explored the logic, reason, and rationale behind the raw food lifestyle and emphasized the intrinsic dangers of cooked food. The main premise of both of my books is that the strong desire to be beautiful is not enough; we must be willing to nurture the only beauty we can ever possess — our own.

Your Right to Be Beautiful will show you how to take advantage of the inseparability of health and beauty after age 40. There are whole chapters on all of the things I ask you to give up forever: sugar, salt, milk, bread, meat, fish, and so on. After you have read the research and understand the negative effects of these foods, you will be even more determined to go raw. Those chapters explain in detail the benefits of the raw food diet in achieving physical attractiveness and how raw, living foods can rejuvenate your body from the inside out. I stress the reasons why certain foods should be avoided.

Your Right to Be Beautiful also features little-known beauty secrets and some basic recipes.

The trip from understanding to appreciating the raw food lifestyle is a fascinating journey. And it is only firsthand experience of the raw food lifestyle that can take you from intellectual knowledge to an intuitive realization of the truth. When this occurs, you will come to a new level of awareness, a new way of being. That is where *Beautiful on Raw* comes in — it helps you to get there. *Your Right to Be Beautiful* tells you why you want to make the journey.

For further help in changing your life, download my eBook: *100 Days to 100% Raw: The Step by Step Guide to the Raw Food Lifestyle for Achieving Optimum Health & Ultimate Beauty*. This eBook features a dynamic, step-by-step curriculum to teach the fundamentals of the raw food lifestyle. These self-facilitated steps will help you kick-start your journey to your superior health and your supreme beauty. It is designed for both newcomers and those seeking to improve their progress.

I plan to constantly update the resources and the day-by-day suggestions in this book. Perhaps, one day I will publish it as a pamphlet that will be available at my seminars. To download *100 Days,* visit my website: *www.BeautifulOnRaw.com.*

I wish you great success in adopting the raw food lifestyle. May you enjoy a Rawsome Life and reveal your own Rawsome Beauty!

Index

If the order form on the following page has already been used, for additional copies of *Your Right to Be Beautiful* and the companion *un*cookbook, *Beautiful On Raw* or *Quantum Eating* order directly from BR Publishing:

online: *www.BeautifulOnRaw.com*
or
by telephone: *(866) STAY-RAW*.

Quick Order Form

Check your leading bookstores for additional copies of *Your Right to Be Beautiful* or the soon to be released *Beautiful On Raw* or order directly from BR Publishing here:

online: *www.BeautifulOnRaw.com*

or

by telephone: *(866) STAY-RAW*

Mail Orders *(please photocopy form):*

BR

BR Publishing
P.O. Box 623
Cordova, TN 38088-0623

Please send me _____ copies of *Your Right to Be Beautiful* @ $20.00 each.

Please send me _____ copies of *Beautiful On Raw* @ $20.00 each.

Please send me _____ copies of *Quantum Eating* @ $30.00 each.

Name: _____

Address: _____

City: _____

State: _____ Zip: _____

Please add $3 per book for shipping.

Payment: Check _____   Money Order _____

Meatless "Meatballs" Nested in Live Macaroni *(p. 212)*

Healthy Buckwheat "Burger" *(p. 214)*

Clever Carrot Cake *(p. 280)*

Fabulous Fruitcake *(p. 288)*

Macadamia Cheese Pie *(p. 282)*

Macadamia Cheese Cake *(p. 282)*

Broccoli Cream Soup *(p. 176)*

Collard Greens Mushroom Soup *(p. 170)*

Meatless "Meatballs" with Red Marinara *(p. 212)*

Red Pecan Crackers with Guacamole *(p. 234)*

New Millennium Salad *(p. 144)*

Stuffed Cherry Tomatoes with Macadamia Cheese *(p. 196)*